W9-ABE-666

The
Witch's Book
of Magical
Ritual

The Witch's Book of Magical Ritual

Use the Forces of Wicca to Direct Your Psychic Powers

Gavin Frost, Ph.D., D.D., and Yvonne Frost, D.D.

REWARD BOOKS

Library of Congress Cataloging-in-Publication Data

Frost, Gavin
    The witch's book of magical ritual / Gavin Frost and Yvonne Frost.
      p. cm.
    Includes bibliographical references and index.
    ISBN 0-7352-0315-6 (alk. paper)
    1. Witchcraft. 2. Ritual. 3. Rites and ceremonies. I. Frost, Yvonne. II. Title.

    BF1566 .F82 2002
    133.4'3—dc21
                                        2002024866

©2003 by Reward Books

All rights reserved. No part of this book may be reproduced in any form or by any means, without permission in writing from the publisher.

Printed in the United States of America

10 9 8 7 6 5 4 3 2 1

ISBN 0-7352-0315-6

ATTENTION: CORPORATIONS AND SCHOOLS
Reward Books are available at quantity discounts with bulk purchase for educational, business, or sales promotional use. For information, please write to: Prentice Hall Special Sales, 240 Frisch Court, Paramus, New Jersey 07652. Please supply: title of book, ISBN, quantity, how the book will be used, date needed.

REWARD BOOKS
Paramus, NJ 07652

✴ DEDICATION ✴

To our daughter Jo, our Golden Girl.

Without her this book could not have been written.

✴ and ✴

To all others who dare to color outside the lines.

Other Books by the Authors

TITLE	PUBLISHED	PUBLISHER
Astral Travel	1986	Weiser
Good Witch's Bible	1991	Godolphin House
Good Witch's Guide to Life	1991	Godolphin House
Helping Yourself with Astromancy	1980	Parker Publishing
Modern Witch's Guide to Beauty, Vigor, and Vitality	1978	Progress Books
Meta-Psychometry	1978	Parker Publishing
Power Secrets from a Sorcerer's Private Magnum Arcanum	1980	Parker Publishing
The Prophet's Bible	1991	Weiser
Tantric Yoga	1989	Weiser
Who Speaks for the Witch?	1991	Godolphin House
Witchcraft: The Way to Serenity	1968	Godolphin House
The Witch's Magical Handbook	2000	Reward
The Magic Power of White Witchcraft	1999	Reward
Witch's Grimoire of Ancient Omens, Portents, Talismans, Amulets, and Charms	1979	Parker Publishing
Witch Words	1993	Godolphin House

Contents

Introduction
Why You Should Pay Attention to This Book xviii

☆ Experience Counts xviii
☆ What This Book Will Do for You xix
☆ Ritual, Spell, Religious Service, Rite, What You Will xx
☆ An Outstanding Success xxi
☆ Everyone Needs a Plan xxi
☆ The Monkey Story xxii
☆ Ritual Procedures xxiii
☆ The Witch's World xxv
☆ Plan and Perform xxv
☆ Roll Up Your Sleeves xxvi

Chapter One
You're Not Supposed to Know You Have Power I

☆ Before We Begin 1
☆ The Classic Experiment 2
☆ Changes in Your Power Output 3
☆ Testing Your Power 3
☆ Making Your Magic Wand 5

☆ The Power of the Wand   6
☆ Inhaling Cosmic Energy   7
☆ Focus Your Power   9
☆ Purpose of the Ritual.   9
☆ Fasting, Celibacy, and Levels of Power   12
☆ Science Explains the Witch's Ritual   12
☆ Becoming Homeostatic   13
☆ The Sequence Is Sacrosanct   14
☆ Edwina, Tim, Janice, Bill.   14
☆ Avoiding the Psychic Vampire   15
☆ Summary   15

CHAPTER TWO
WHY BOTHER?   17

☆ Why.   17
☆ The Last Resort   17
☆ First Things First.   18
☆ Eddie L Cures Himself.   20
☆ Eddie's Ritual Plan   22
☆ Reasons for Ritual   22
   ☆ Money.   23
   ☆ Companionship   23
   ☆ Healing   25
   ☆ Serenity.   25
   ☆ Protection   26
☆ Ho Hum, or Urgent Necessity?   26
☆ Jo Cures Eli's Sprained Ankle   27
☆ Witches Heal the Earth   28
☆ Choosing Where to Put the Magical Energy   29
☆ Yes, but Bert Wasted Two Weeks and a Thousand Dollars   34
☆ What This Chapter Shows You.   36
☆ What This Book Shows You   36

CHAPTER THREE
WHAT DO YOU REALLY WANT?   37

☆ Living Someone Else's Dream? 37

☆ Lottery Winners Are Losers. 38
☆ Quality of Life 39
☆ Edwina and Her Range Rover   42
☆ There's Nowt So Queer as Folks.   43
☆ Where Will You Be in a Decade?   46
   ☆ Location   46
   ☆ Housing.   47
   ☆ Companionship.   48
   ☆ Career.   48
☆ Greg and His Journey   49
☆ "Longest Journey Starts with Single Step".   50
☆ Affirmations and Questions.   50
☆ How Jerry the Trained Occultist Screwed Up   52

CHAPTER FOUR
HOW MUCH POWER DO YOU NEED?   55

☆ Katya's Dream Works.   55
☆ Targeting   56
☆ Optimal Use of Power   57
☆ Distance Makes a Difference   58
☆ Mona and the Bishop   59
☆ Target Timing.   61
☆ Alicia's Spell Finally Worked   62
☆ Tune Your Psychic Radio   63
☆ The Web of the Wyrd   65
☆ Modifying Your Intent   66
☆ Conclusion   67

CHAPTER FIVE
ENHANCING THE HIGH   69

☆ Cautionary Tales   69
☆ Mind Keys   69
☆ Ritual Objects   72
☆ Mind Keys and Emotion   74

☆ Use All Your Senses   75
☆ Diamond Got Worse   75
☆ Psychic Links   76
☆ Crystals   78
☆ Tricia Moves Back to Arkansas   79
☆ The Powers in Metals and Woods   80
☆ Your Guide to the Powers of Crystals,
   Metals, and Woods   80
☆ Herbs   81
☆ Finding the Power of Psychic Transmitters   81
☆ Summary   82

Chapter Six
Magical Tools and Location   85

☆ Your Magician's Tools   85
   ☆ Consumables and Equipment for Your Ritual   85
   ☆ Basic Requirements   86
   ☆ The Sacred Measure   87
   ☆ The Altar   88
   ☆ The Robe   89
   ☆ The Athame   89
   ☆ Selecting Your Secret Name and Number   92
   ☆ Making the Book of Light   93
   ☆ The Chalice and Bowls   93
   ☆ Consumables   93
   ☆ Making Mead   94
   ☆ Candles and Holders   96
   ☆ Cleaning Equipment of Psychic Noise   96
☆ Location, Location, Location   96
   ☆ Geomancy   97
   ☆ Places of Power   98
   ☆ Map Dowsing   98
   ☆ Ley Lines   98
   ☆ Manufacturing Your Own Power Points   99
   ☆ Far from the Madding Crowd   99
   ☆ Cho Hoi Moves from His House   101

☆ Eddie, Charlayne, and Brushwood   101
☆ Legal Occupancy   102
☆ Your Location: Finding a Site   103
☆ Conclusion   104

Chapter Seven
Timing   105

☆ Full Moon, Dark Sun   105
☆ Moon Phases   107
☆ Wynne Died of a Tonsillectomy   109
☆ Deana and Her Refrigerator   109
☆ Astrological Misinformation   110
☆ Energy from Beyond the Stars   111
☆ Filling In Your Work Sheet   113
☆ A Note to Amateur Astrologers   116
☆ Getting High at the Right Time   117
☆ Rituals for Special Dates   118
☆ When Their Guard Is Down   119
☆ Conclusion   119

Chapter Eight
The Big Four   121

☆ Universal Quests   121
☆ Companionship   122
    ☆ The Ethics of Companionship Rituals   122
    ☆ Defining the Intent   122
☆ Wealth   125
    ☆ Materialism and the Web   125
    ☆ Defining the Intent   125
☆ Health   127
    ☆ The Karma of Healing   127
    ☆ Defining the Healing Intents   127
☆ Protection   129
☆ Have You Been Hexed?   129
☆ Understanding the Forces Against You   130

☆ Your Protective Mirror   131
☆ Bill, Sam, and the New Freeway   132
☆ Your Gods of the Six Directions   133
☆ Your Psychic Second Line of Defense   136
☆ Talismans to Guard the Holes in Your Defense   136
  ☆ Protecting the Brain and the Head   137
  ☆ Protecting the Heart and the Throat   138
  ☆ The Hands   138
  ☆ Your Psychic Chastity Belt   139
  ☆ Protecting Your Feet   139
  ☆ Protecting Your Navel   139
☆ Attack: The Best Form of Defense   140
☆ Protecting All Phases of Your Life   140
☆ God Talks to George   141
☆ Buy a Ticket   141

Chapter Nine
Getting Your Ducks in a Row   143

☆ Raising and Directing Power   143
☆ Your God Bargain   144
☆ Constructing Your Ritual Space   145
☆ Your Circle of Containment   146
☆ Your Circle of Protection   146
☆ Your Holy Space   148
☆ Steps Beyond   148
☆ Your Ritual Flow   150
☆ Your Ritual Work Sheets   152
☆ Longest Path, Shortest Time   154
☆ Your RAPT Chart   155
☆ Bobbie Jean Disqualifies Herself   156
☆ This Is Not a Democracy   157
☆ Alternatives Are Okay   158
☆ The Last Three Days of the World as You Knew It . . .   158
☆ Don't Panic   160

CHAPTER TEN
THE MASTER RITUAL   161

☆ Today's the Day   161
☆ Remember Ritual Order   162
☆ The Master Ritual Format   163
☆ Time for Ritual   164
☆ "Not Applicable" Is Not an Answer   171

CHAPTER ELEVEN
WHAT HAPPENED?   173

☆ Something Did Too Happen   173
☆ Brad's Father Wins the Lottery   174
☆ The Law of Silence   174
☆ Errors in Ritual Lead to Strange Results   175
☆ The Timing of the Results   177
☆ Analysis and Desire versus Reality   178
☆ Why and How Did Lavinia Get Her New Car?   178
☆ The Line of Least Resistance   180
☆ Was the Trade-off Worth It?   181
☆ Real Results or Coincidence?   182
☆ Change Takes Time   183
☆ Don't Just Walk Away   184
☆ Today's Errors, Tomorrow's Success   185

CHAPTER TWELVE
YOUR RITUAL LIFE   187

☆ Where Are You in Your Life?   187
☆ Making Your Habits Work for You   189
☆ Amanda and Ted Remarry   191
☆ Single versus Group   192
☆ If It Harm None   195
☆ Your Value Set   196
☆ Eddie, Randy, Jeanne, and Garnet Break Out   197

☆ Forming Your Own Group   199
☆ Planning Your Future Ritual Life   199

Appendix One: Tables   201

1 Disease-Color Correspondence   201
2 Master Meta-Psychometric Table   202
3 Botanical Names of Flowers and Herbs   204
4 Mind Triggers for Seven Intents   205
5 Natural Sources of Energy for Seven Intents   206

Appendix Two:
Legal Implications of Joining
a Witch Group   207

Index of Tables, Figures, and Work Sheets   213
Index   217

Introduction

Why You Should Pay Attention to This Book

The other day at a book signing session, we heard the request, "I want a book that tells me how to *do* it! I guess I want a super spell book." This is that book—a book of practical magic, with few or no spiritual and religious overtones.

This book will enable you to write a ritual and perform it so that you can manifest anything in your life that you wish. Whether you write it alone or with co-workers, the ritual will inherently have more power than any predigested ritual you might find in a "spell book." Because you will understand the ingredients, the sequence, and the technique before you perform the ritual, you will be assured of the results you desire.

The authors combine more experience of actually living Witchcraft and its associated rituals than anyone else. More than thirty years ago we founded a correspondence school for Witches.

In those years we have guided over 40,000 students, worldwide, along the Wiccan path.[1] We the authors were Witches before we founded the correspondence school. Our combined associated life in the Craft amounts to over eighty years.

In conjunction with our students we have designed hundreds of rituals—and through the students' work we know the results of well over 100,000 actual workings—many good, but a few that turned out to have either amusing or catastrophic results. As you go through the book you will read about some successes and some near misses. We may have learned more from those near misses than from perfectly completed procedures.

Experience Counts

Not long ago we tried to compute the number of rituals we have attended and designed. The total came to a little over 1,000. We thought hard about the half-dozen that went disastrously wrong; we contrasted those with the hundreds that went well and achieved their intended results. We realized that a simple planning book would benefit today's "alternative" community. Such a book would help avoid the more glaring flaws to which rituals are susceptible.

Few if any members of the alternative community can claim our experience in Wiccan magical ritual. Certainly none have the decades of experience in teaching others to design and perform successful rituals.

The advantage of having a large student body of newcomers to the Craft (neophytes) is this: They can conduct psychic experiments largely without preconceived notions that might have infected them from the many trash books on the market. As a simple example of this, after casting so many circles we can clearly define the best size, the best shape, and the best materials to arrive at the optimal circle.

---

[1] *Wicca* is the name we use for the spiritual path of Witchcraft. We follow that spiritual path, and in 1972 we earned federal recognition for it. To read more about the Church of Wicca and the courses we teach, see the Web at http://www.wicca.org.

Workers raise *real* power in circle. You may have learned from our other books how to experience it. The power that goes out does not disappear. It finds a home. It may accomplish the desired task or something similar; or it may wreak an inner change in you, the practitioner. Be sure, though, that something *will* happen—future events will alter their course.

When a ritual succeeds, the change appears. In some cases, perhaps a healing, this *outer* change is most apparent; moreover, whether the healing "worked" or not, a change occurs in the practitioner. A healing may not cure the patient's disease in the conventional sense—though at very least the patient obtains serenity and enough strength to face the future. Such a healing makes as much emotional change as it does physical.

Sometimes very little change seems to occur in the practitioner, as when we work to heal a third party. At other times, as in a companionship ritual, the inner change immediately shows. Make no mistake: Every action results in a reaction. The more thought, energy, and intensity goes into a ritual, the more reliable are the results.

What This Book Will Do for You

If you have read about Witches and the Craft, you may know the thing(s) you need to do to make something happen. The simple ritual of an unskilled worker has a low chance of success; as we say, the more you put into it, the more likely it is to succeed. The complex rituals you have read about may seem daunting. This book enables you to put the facts that you have learned into a rational, effective framework. Then your ritual becomes successful and easy to perform. If you like, think of this book as a cookbook, not for food, but for spells.

> You do not have to be an initiated Witch to make the ritual format in this book work, any more than you have to be a blue-ribbon chef to use a cookbook.

If you were baking a solstice cake[2] without a cookbook, you might well omit the spices that make the cake so flavorful. Occasionally we attend rituals conducted by leaders of the Wiccan community and find that through carelessness they have omitted vital steps. Even Wiccan leaders could use a planning guide like this book.

> It matters not what your religious affiliation. You can use this recipe book to produce a ritual in any religious context. What if you are a Christian and wish to manifest something in your life? You can benefit from this book as much as the Wiccan who wants to affect the future or the Shinto priest who wants to bring fertility to the crops.

Worldwide, human beings have the same powers, no matter what their skin color or official religion. They feel similar needs. They express similar emotions. Similar mind triggers turn them on. The Great Mother Goddess image prevails. Many new workers succeed as well as, if not better than, old-timers. The many easily completed work sheets in this book guide you to doing successful, smooth-running rituals. It matters not whether you work solitary or in a group; nor does it matter whether you aim for serenity, for wealth, for companionship, or for any other purpose.

RITUAL, SPELL, RELIGIOUS SERVICE, RITE, WHAT YOU WILL

With bated breath outsiders accuse Witches of "doing spells" using herbal potions and noxious substances. Yet in a communion service, the priest does a spell to commute bread and wine into flesh and blood. Call it what you will—religious service, spell, or ritual—it's all the same thing. Sometimes the doctor's medicines taste just as unpleasant as the herbal potions that many of us now take under the label of nutritional supplements.

---

[2]Usually December 22, the great winter solstice festival usurped by the Roman Catholic Church As Christ-mass.

Ritual—The performance of a spell or a religious service to a known format.

Spell—Formula of incantation or discourse. It is no long etymological stretch from *good spell* to *god spell* to *gospel*.

Religious Service—A ritual performed for reassurance.

Rite—A formal procedure or act.

An Outstanding Success

Six people in a meadow at midnight, working in a magical circle, dancing sky-clad[3] under the moon, raising power, chanting, finally screaming out their intent, "Heal!" They meant it from their hearts. They put their all into it. After the ritual the participants felt so deflated, drained, limp, that they knew the procedure had worked. Within three days they learned that their target—a single mother of two young children—had recovered from life-threatening leukemia.

The doctors called it "spontaneous remission"; but we who live and work in the Craft know that such alleged spontaneous remissions often follow when Witches work to heal.

Everyone Needs a Plan

> The unexamined life is not worth living.[4]
> The unplanned Ritual is not worth doing.

This book contains explicit, real-world information on ways to make anything you desire manifest in your life. When you use it in conjunction with *The Magic Power of White Witchcraft* and *The Witch's Magical Handbook*, you can design and accomplish for yourself rituals that are extraordinarily powerful, dynamic, and effective. Your every wish can become *real*. In these two books we covered many

---

[3]Sky-clad: without clothing or bindings on the body.
[4]Plato, *Apology*

quite advanced systems for raising power and for channeling. A little of that material is repeated in this book for the sake of completeness. We strongly recommend that you read those two books if you want to get further understanding of real magic. Here we build on the basics to guide you in using them to produce successful rituals.

The Monkey Story

There's an old story about a monkey. One day its master left it in the car with the keys in the ignition. The monkey jumped up and down on the back seat for a few moments, then decided it had to go to the bathroom, so it did that. Then it climbed into the front seat and played with the controls. Finally it turned on the ignition and made the windshield wipers work. It rolled the windows down and up again. Then—purely by chance—it turned on the radio and got some music that it liked.

The next time it got left in the car, the monkey remembered the music it had enjoyed. It jumped up and down on the back seat for a moment, went to the bathroom, climbed into the front seat, played with the controls. It turned on the ignition; the windshield wipers worked; the windows went down and back up. It turned on the radio, and music played. (voila!)

It told several of its monkey friends how to do it. Its procedure became monkey law, passed on for generations. Needless to say there was a rash of spoiled back seats.

This little story illustrates several very important points in constructing your rituals.

1. Many available books will give you very complex instructions for doing a ritual. If you follow the instructions with perfect accuracy, you may get the results they promise. You don't have to have any understanding of what you are doing or why, and many of the actions you go through are not necessary to get the result you want.

2. Similarly if another monkey tells you how to do something, be sure that the recommended procedure has been tested. Don't make yourself a guinea pig. All too often self-appointed experts have tried a ritual only once and have lucked out.

3. The fact that Grandma and Grandpa did it a certain way doesn't necessarily mean it's the right and only way.

4. Check your sources. Even though a particular schism of the Golden Dawn did it in a certain way, and even though St. Gerald Gardner picked up some of those ways, and even though others picked up Gardner's ways, even all that doesn't mean that it's the best way.

We think we have the best way—for us; but that may not mean it's the best way for *you*. We've tried our best to eliminate all unnecessary steps; but a couple may still have crept through. Always do your rituals with understanding of what each step is meant to accomplish. When you use one of our rituals, if you find you can do it in a way that is as effective but more efficient,

tell us.

Over the more than three decades we've been teaching, we've worked hard to lower the obfuscation index; but we are sure there is room for improvement—if we but knew it. Common sense (that uncommon virtue) tells you that if we don't know about it, we can't fix it.

If antiquity does not make it right, and the author does not make it right, if a friend whispering in your ear doesn't make it right, what does? Choose a ritual and try it for yourself. If it *works*, and if it's *ethical*, that's what makes it right.

Ritual Procedures

The more you ritualize the routine actions of your life, the easier it becomes to live in the ever-more-complex world of the twenty-first century. If you lead the busy life that so many do today, the ritualizing of your morning shower, your breakfast, and your commute to work increases efficiency. It is simply more efficient to follow a plan than to reinvent the wheel every morning. In talking about ritual work, we mean beginning with such simple acts as cleaning your teeth and getting dressed in the morning. Then move on to the more complex magical rituals designed to alter future events and to manifest in your life all that you desire.

A typical age-old spell that children still recite is:

> Rain, rain, go away.
> Come again another day.
> Little Jennie wants to play.

In ancient times ritual permeated and defined people's lives. Before printed texts were widely available, and certainly before the age of the Internet, people needed ritual if they were to know how and when to do things. Ritual ranged from such acts as planting the crops to performing the duties of a midwife. The little rituals preserving hard-won knowledge were easy to remember, and were passed down so that essential work could be carried out in useful and effective ways. Taking an overview of this aspect of oral history, the world we know has lost such ritualization. We feel this is a very negative aspect of modern living. Oral traditions and family time to preserve history or the telling of stories still have value today.

In today's world our stages of life have become degraded, transformed into pretexts for worshiping at the money shrine. A birthday does not celebrate the birth of the person or show gratitude for Mother's support; instead it is an excuse to buy more, bigger, "better" presents. Puberty rituals similarly fail the participants. Coming of age now implies being able to drink and to drive the flashy new car that Daddy bought. These attitudes ignore an acceptance and understanding of one's place in society, in Nature, and in the universe. The "Christian" Western world has almost totally abandoned definitive coming-of-age rituals.

THE WITCH'S WORLD

A Witch's life is bounded—defined—by ritual. Beyond regular services and circles, she[5] tends also to ritualize the routine acts of everyday life. Many a Witch spends a few moments each morning acknowledging her gratitude to the Mother and to life itself. She

---

[5]The overwhelming number of women who died in the Wiccan Holocaust makes the use of the female gender more than politically correct. Today about 60 percent of Wiccans are women.

acknowledges her place within the scheme of Nature. Through such acts she gives meaning to every day.

A Witch acknowledges the ever-changing seasons with rituals keyed to the occasion. Yes, many Witches succumb to the birthday-present syndrome; most of us also teach our children to be grateful for real things, not for the ephemeral trinket *du jour*. In other words, ritual gives children strong keys to the stages of their lives and to the cycles of Nature.

PLAN AND PERFORM

Without planning, rituals often go awry. Even the simplest ritual deserves careful thinking through. Admittedly, if you anticipate conducting a large public ritual that many newcomers will attend, the logistics need detail-by-detail organizing. Such an event is more challenging to manage than a private ritual attended by only one or two experienced people.

We have seen high priest/esses in small rituals simply forget major steps. They fail to have at hand the supplies and artifacts essential to perform the ritual smoothly and effectively. It's almost a joke—an unfortunate one—in the pagan/Wiccan community that if something does not go wrong, it isn't a good ritual. We tolerate no defense of such an attitude. We don't say that every T must be crossed and every word pronounced by rote. A responsible high priest/ess who does his or her job properly does not skip steps or suddenly realize that a vital ingredient is missing. A little planning is a wonderful thing.

Anyone who wants to do a ritual can use this book. Sometimes we compare doing a ritual to cooking. To boil an egg you need simple equipment, but you need all the tools. You need a stove and a saucepan. To cook a major Thanksgiving dinner, you must add more equipment and planning. Don't forget your cookbook. When you want to do a ritual don't forget this book.

Roll Up Your Sleeves

We offer a straightforward premise: Decide the following options one by one:

R eward for your work—what is it?
I dentify effort.
T riggers and supplies.
U se timing and charts.
A ct.
L og your outcome and meditation.

Remember the RITUAL for doing a ritual!

The reward of many rituals today is the smiling good health of the target person. Sometimes the reward is of immediate value in your own life, as in the unexpected gift of money or objects of desire. It may be a new lifelong companion. It may be greater spiritual understanding.

Remember: Longest journey begins with single step.

It's simple. It's easy. It's fun. It's rewarding.

Read it—Understand it—DO IT.

Chapter One

Your're Not Supposed to Know You Have Power

Before We Begin[1]

In order to set the stage and be sure we are all working from the same basic knowledge, this chapter reviews some ideas about the occult power you will use in your rituals. If you have read our earlier books, go directly to Chapter Two.

Everyone has the ability within themselves to put out psychic energy. That energy has been known for centuries. Hindus call it *prana*. In martial arts it is *chi*. Germans call it *vril*. Since George Lucas' *Star Wars*, people call it *the Force*. Scientists call it *bioplasmic energy*. The Oxford Dictionary defines it as,

> Vril: a natural wonder-working force.

University researchers are actively researching what the Force can do. It is no longer something to scoff at. They know that people

---

[1]Some of the sections following and illustrations are excerpted from *The Witch's Magical Handbook* and *The Magic Power of White Witchcraft*. They are placed here for completeness.

can fog photographic film—and put pictures on film.[2] They know that psychic energy can deform metal objects and move heavy weights.

Over literally centuries of exploration and testing, people have learned how to maximize the Force they can put out as an individual, and how to raise the Force in a group. As you read on, you will learn to maximize your own Force and to tune it so that you send it out in a form best thought of as a laser beam which can penetrate through space and through material objects to do your bidding.

The Classic Experiment

You need not take our word for any of this. You can witness for yourself the fact that the power is real. When you next stand in line at the checkout counter, look along the line and find someone who is daydreaming. Put out the thought, "Look around!" When you do this regularly, more and more often the person whom you attempt to reach will, in fact, be affected and will turn around to stare at you.

This is a simple telepathic demonstration of the power that has been in you since birth. As you sit and read this book you are not standing in line at the supermarket, so an even simpler demonstration can show you that power is within you. Hold up your left hand, as shown in Figure I-1, and point the fingers of the right hand at the palm of the left. Keep the fingertips about one inch from the left palm.[3]

Now slowly move your entire right forearm, passing the fingers up and down past the palm of the left hand as the arrows of Figure I-1 show. You should feel a kind of breeze or lightness or a tingle as the fingers move past the palm. That is your life force. It is the energy field, the effect of which can be photographed in a technique called Kirilian photography. That field is symptomatic of the power that you can send out to influence others.

Now you have felt your basic power.

---

[2]By dictionary definition the fogging of photographic negatives or pictures is usually the result of exposure to light; however, some people are able to cause this blurring of the image or producing fog-like images on film with their minds. The most astounding case of actually putting pictures on film was studied by Professor Jule Eisenbud, M.D., and is reported in *The World of Ted Serios: "Thoughtographic" Studies of an Extraordinary Mind* (William Morrow, 1967).

[3]If you are left-handed, point the fingers of the left hand at the palm of the right.

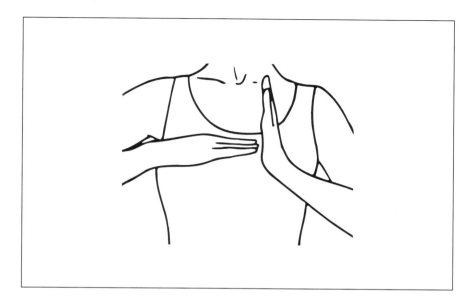

Figure I-1
Feeling Your Own Power

CHANGES IN YOUR POWER OUTPUT

When you try to demonstrate the energy field to a friend, he may not be able to feel it. This can happen when your "vibes are low." The strength of your power will vary depending on your physical condition and on the time of day. If you don't feel a sensation now, try it at about ten o'clock on Sunday morning after an unhurried breakfast. It is no coincidence that many conventional churches hold services at this time, when they want to raise power.

TESTING YOUR POWER

To demonstrate the different levels of power as they vary through-out the day, spend a day testing your energy. When you first wake in the morning, try the fingers-across-palm experiment. It may be difficult to feel anything. As the morning progresses, though, gradually the field will become more definite. If you eat a heavy lunch, soon after the meal the sensation will weaken again, but will become more perceptible as digestive activity slows and energy becomes available from the food.

Experiment at the times of day listed in the left-hand column of Work Sheet I-1. Enter a check mark in the appropriate weak/average/strong column.[4]

The classic experiment described here is quite subjective. It is not something you clock on a meter. If you want to get more scientific in your experiments, look at Chapter One of *The Witch's Magical Handbook*. There you will find experiments with a Crookes radiometer; those are more definitive.

Hour of Day	Weak	Average	Strong
1 a.m.			
3 a.m.			
5 a.m.			
7 a.m.			
9 a.m.			
11 a.m.			
1 p.m.			
3 p.m.			
5 p.m.			
7 p.m.			
9 p.m.			
11 p.m.			

Work Sheet I-1
Testing Your Power

---

[4]We strongly recommend that you avoid writing on the actual pages of this book. Copy a given work sheet and use that copy as your working draft. Workers have found that they may need several work copies of a chart, and it is sensible to keep the original pages clean.

Making Your Magic Wand

To investigate the power further, you need a way of concentrating its effect. Everyone has heard of the magician with his magic wand, and a properly made wand does indeed concentrate and focus the power.

There are many designs for wands; but in our opinion, those presently on the market seem to concentrate on being pretty. Of course their design may include crystals and other jewels; unfortunately pretty doesn't hack it. So far none of these wands we've seen has worked as well as our old-fashioned simple one. Figure I-2 shows how to construct a good wand. Traditionally the iron rod has been inserted by burning its way in; however, you may find this procedure difficult to accomplish. In the ancient instructions the wood is from a lightning-struck tree; in this case you will find that the center of the wood has been carbonized. If you are lucky enough to find such wood, you can omit the iron rod.

We mere mortals usually use a piece of wood from a broom or mop handle, and drill through it to insert the iron rod. An alternative is to cut a dowel into sections lengthwise and drill each section individually; then reassemble and glue the pieces together onto the rods with a good grade of plastic glue. Do not use a water-soluble glue, for occasionally you will want to cleanse your wand psychically by boiling.

The use of one-eighth inch silver rod is very important. Do not skimp in this area of your wand-making. We have successfully used one-eighth inch copper instead of silver; however, the silver is definitely preferable. The spaces between the turns should be such that when you hold the rod in your hand, your fingers fit comfortably between them. In use, the forefinger lies along the silver bar that points toward the tip of the wand.

In the same way you felt the energy from your fingertips, you can now feel the way your wand focuses energy. Hold the wand in your primary hand and point it at the palm of your receiving (secondary) hand; you will feel a spot of energy. Now do the same research with time of day and energy levels that you did before, now holding the wand for each trial, and find the time(s) when your Force peaks. Enter your findings in a copy of Work Sheet I-1.

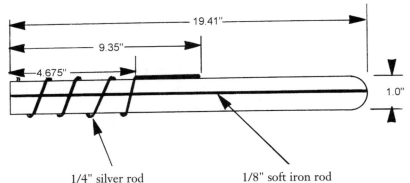

1/4" silver rod   1/8" soft iron rod
(The silver rod is a single continuous piece 18" long.) Use wood approximately 1"
in diameter. Doweling or a section of broom handle can be used. Varnish with six
coats of marine varnish.

Figure I-2
Your Magic Wand

THE POWER OF THE WAND

The wand is a powerful magical tool that directs the Force to your
chosen target. Do not lightly point it at people, and never ever point
it at anyone's eyes. To see its power for yourself, do the following
"Interruption" experiment. From those earlier experiments, choose
a time when your power is high; place the objects listed in the left
column of Work Sheet I-2 between the tip of the wand and the palm
of your receiving hand.

Interruption	Level of Feeling		
	Weak	Average	Strong
a. Book, 1/2" thick			
b. Book, 1½" thick			
c. As in b. with foil placed in center			
d. As in c. with additional foil at end			
e. 1/2" steel plate			
f. Thin leather			
g. Glass or bottle of water			

Work Sheet I-2
The Interruption Experiment

Inhaling Cosmic Energy

The technique of inhaling cosmic energy is age-old. It involves assuming the Star Position shown in Figure I-3. Tilt your head slightly backward to align the spine to the most effective position so that the power can flow more freely. In Figure I-3 the right palm is up and the left palm down. Try it both ways, once as shown and once the other way, with the *left* palm up and *right* palm down.

Stand up now and assume the Star Position. After a moment or so you will feel one palm growing cool and the other warm. Quickly turn your hands over (reverse the direction each palm is facing) to prove that the temperature sensation is something external and actual, not imagined, and that you are genuinely interrupting the flow of a power field. As you let the power flow through you, every few moments repeat the wand or fingers-across-palm experiment. You will feel the sensation gradually build up. For some reason that we do not yet understand, when you assume the Star Position and let the energy flow through you, some energy stays with you. It is as though you were a pipe with water flowing through it; the pipe remains damp even when the flow stops.

Now you have proven to yourself that you can feel the power flowing through you. Knowing this, you can make yourself into a great cosmic accumulator. Visualize the flow of infinite cosmic energy rushing past you as a blue-white light. Hear it as a wind in the treetops.

Stand in the Star Position. First the energy will flow in through your hand and upward into your head. Some of it will also enter through the fontanelle, the "soft spot" at the top of the skull where the infant bones grow together in the months after birth. Feel the coolness of the breeze. You are going to fill your body with cosmic energy. You will feel your head come alive and glow and pulse with energy. Let the head fill with energy. Then bring the power down through the throat and heart into the abdomen. Visualize the energy flowing down to the solar plexus; feel the momentary unsettled condition of your stomach as you fill these lower areas. Imagine infinite power filling you as water would fill you. Finally, bring it down into your genitalia. As you fill this area you will feel your physical organs vibrate and tingle. Do not be uneasy; that very natural feeling will be dispersed when you send the power to your chosen target.

Now you are full of cosmic energy. To a clairvoyant, you would glow in the dark; and a Kirilian photograph of your hand would show a tremendous stream of light/energy flowing from it. Russian experimenters have even recorded the crackling noises of the discharge as one of their well-known healers filled himself with energy and sent that energy into the body of his patient.

Figure I-3
The Star Position

Focus Your Power

Now that you have learned to build your power and have observed the time of day when it is strongest, you will want to learn to send the power out on a specific errand. You know that it flows out the end of your wand, so it makes sense to point the wand in the direction of the target person or thing to be influenced.

One characteristic of the Force that seems to be little understood is that it is *tuneable.* Just as you tune a radio to get the station you want, so you tune the Force to do the task you want it to do. Imagine if you like, that instead of the radio tuning in various stations, it tunes in various *intents.* At one end of the dial there might be *Love,* at the other *Attack;* and as you go along the dial you may find such options as *Healing, Luck,* and other intents that may help you in a spell to fulfill your dream. Later chapters suggest specific mind keys that will tune you to the intent you want to bring about.

Purpose of the Ritual

The purpose of a ritual is to make sure that the outgoing energy is

a. at as high a level as possible;

b. correctly tuned to the intent; and

c. done at the most effective time and in the most effective place.

To this point we have addressed the *single* practitioner. Now let's think about two or more people working together. Observers have long known that in doing a given spell, two people of opposite psychic gender working together are capable of raising more energy than two people of the same psychic gender. Our research convinces us that the optimal group is usually around six workers, especially if such a group is in "perfect pairs"—if it consists of pairs of people in perfect psychic-gender balance: for every male spirit working, a female spirit, and vice versa.[5] In larger groups we find that getting everyone tuned to the same specific intent is difficult.

---

[5]Here we are dealing with the gender of the *spirit.* In decidedly heterosexual people, spiritual gender is usually the same as physical gender. In homosexuals it may or may not be the same as the physical gender. Hence our use of the inclusive term *psychic gender.*

About twenty years ago Dr. Loy Stone (then president of the Church of Wicca) investigated the magnetic fields surrounding living organisms. He encased the organism (or in humans just the head) in a very large coil of super-fine wire; then he connected the output of the coil to a galvanometer. He found that most males would deflect the galvanometer one way, and most females would deflect it in the opposite direction.

You can see that if people have opposite magnetic or electrical polarities, then working together would be like connecting two batteries in series; whereas people with the same polarity working together would resemble two batteries in parallel. In other words, as Figure I-4 shows, you will get double the voltage out of the batteries in series that you will get from the batteries in parallel.

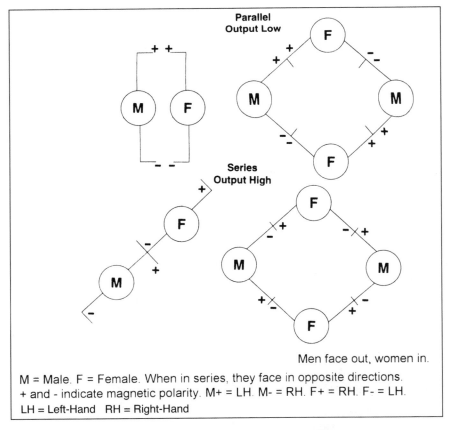

Men face out, women in.

M = Male. F = Female. When in series, they face in opposite directions.
+ and - indicate magnetic polarity. M+ = LH. M- = RH. F+ = RH. F- = LH.
LH = Left-Hand   RH = Right-Hand

Figure I-4 — Series Gives Maximum Force

To feel that energy for yourself, do a modified hands-across-palm experiment, what we call a diadic Force experiment. Stand facing another person. Put your right hand with fingers parallel, palm down, over his left hand. Then place your left hand with its palm up under his right hand with its palm down. You will feel either a flow of strong energy or very little energy. The surge occurs, of course, when your coworker is of the same gender or if the person is of the opposite gender but the hands are crossed. Figure I-5 shows this experiment. In mixed-gender groups, your balance improves when you have an equal number of opposite polarities. In the old texts, the men always faced outward from the center and the women inward. You can see from Figure I-5 how such an arrangement strengthens the Force. Here, contrary to all the stereotypes, holding hands is a no-no. The Force is polarized *parallel* to the fingers, so with the fingers crossed as in holding hands, the power switches off.

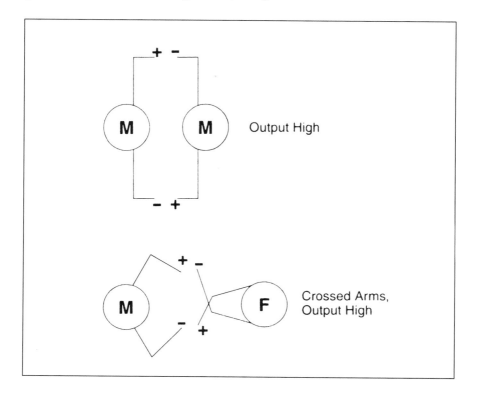

Figure I-5—Diadic Force

Fasting, Celibacy, and Levels of Power

In order to raise power, the workers must be involved in the project, must be in agreement with the intent, and must have a high level of excitement. Sitting around hoping vaguely that something will happen does not do it; instead you must get up on your hind legs, dance, clap, yell, whatever, and get excited.

Science Explains the Witch's Ritual

For centuries people dabbling in the "occult," and Witches, experimented to find methods that would consistently produce results. Only relatively recently have scientists confirmed that the techniques we employ in ritual change the human body at the cellular level—in ways that make possible great power output, meditation, and astral travel. Only recently has quantifiable proof come from dispassionate observers of Craft and magical practices.

To send power out, the worker needs to be involved and excited. It seems that the level of power is directly related to levels of adrenaline in the worker's body. Professor Hans Selye's[6] work has shown that when the body is stressed, levels of adrenaline rise.

One of the most severe bodily stressors is a strict diet—a fast. When such a diet is followed by a requirement to work in the middle of the night, more stress/distress is added. Some groups add further stress through various so-called "tests of manhood" or "dedication" involving actual physical risks. Another stressor that can be added is becoming celibate. Our group uses both fasting and celibacy to increase our power.[7] All these stressors combine with a

---

[6]Hans Selye, *The Stress of Life* (McGraw Hill, 1978).
[7]Tables of stressors are available on the web at www.WebMD.com. The most famous, and the one we use, was composed by Drs. Holmes and Rahe at the University of Washington Medical School.

final exciting chant to get the adrenaline high essential to the sending-out of power. To test yourself, do the hands-across-palm response at the same time each day, and record the results in Work Sheet I-3.

Time	Weak	Average	Strong
Immediately after a meal			
24 hours later (after fasting and being celibate)			
48 hours later (after fasting and being celibate)			
60 hours later (after fasting and being celibate)			

Work Sheet I-3
Testing the Effect of Fasting and Celibacy

The majority of results show that immediately after a meal, your power levels are low. The power level rises day by day until it seems to maximize for most people after the third day of fasting and celibacy.

BECOMING HOMEOSTATIC

To get into the homeostatic state needed for meditation and astral travel, *grounding* needs to occur. At the cellular level the body must be changed away from the adrenaline high to a receptive state. The first step here is a pause of at least fifteen minutes. Then the worker must generate the various peptides (mainly endorphins) that will lock into the opiate receptors at the cellular level[8] to prepare the body for the meditative and astral experience. The generation of these peptides rapidly following the adrenaline high minimizes any physical damage caused by excessive adrenaline in the system.

Several methods may serve to stimulate the essential peptides. Meditation, drumming, exercise, slow dancing, and the chanting of a mantra are all useful. The one that generates the highest level of endorphins is an orgasm.

---

[8]Candace Pert, Ph.D., *Molecules of Emotion* (Simon and Schuster, 1997).

The Tantric experience shows that orgasm is the easiest and quickest method; if that is not possible or conflicts with the religious principles of the worker, another method can be tried. In his best-selling book *The Relaxation Response*, Professor Benson suggests various methods.[9]

THE SEQUENCE IS SACROSANCT

The key here is that you cannot change the order of the ritual—the sequence of events. Coming to the ritual already stressed, adding more stress to get on the adrenaline high, then finally the relaxing that makes the body produce the necessary peptides—this is a logical, effective, scientifically proven sequence of events, not something that can be toyed with. Nor, we would like to add, is it some off-the-wall arbitrary gasping new-age system designed to puff a guru's ego. Although the scientific proof is new, the system is millennia old.

EDWINA, TIM, JANICE, BILL

These four young people live in San Francisco. While they were students at UC–Berkeley, they had read one of our books. In a motorcycle spill, Edwina's brother Tyler scraped a huge area of skin off his buttocks and back. The students decided they would work to heal him. With very litttle preparation, they got together, danced, and yelled out their intent. Very little happened. Being persistent, they backtracked and did the one-on-one experiments. To their surprise, Tim seemed to act like a black hole. Any time he tried the hands-across-palm experiment with the two girls, nothing happened.

They called us about their findings. We told them that some people—whether through strong early religious training, or through unexpressed skepticism, we couldn't tell—were in fact absorbers, not transmitters. The term in "alternative" circles for this is *psychic vam-*

---

[9]Herbert Benson, M.D., *The Relaxation Response* (Avon, 1975).

pire. Whether consciously or unconsciously, they draw energy from others—but put none out. We told them quite frankly we have no idea how to fix it. We suggested that Edwina and Bill do the ritual, leaving Janice and Tim out.

Their work was immediately successful. Perfect scabbing began to occur on Tyler's body. Very soon the incredulous doctors decided they did not need to do the extensive skin transplants they had envisioned. Only one area seemed as if it would not recover. Tyler was not circumcised, and the doctors successfully used segements of his foreskin to repair that area.

Avoiding the Psychic Vampire

Avoiding psychic vampires both in your temporal life and in your ritual work becomes important when you open up your awareness. You will find that some people, perhaps in the workplace or in family gatherings, just simply drain you. Being with them leaves you totally depleted and depressed. Try getting them to do the hands-across-palm experiment with you. Right away you will be able to tell whether they are sucking your energy or whether they are putting energy out. In most cases you will find that these people are sucking up your energy. You need to defend yourself against such individuals. You need protective rings on your hands and perhaps a protective amulet on your breast.[10]

Summary

You have power. Further, nearly all your friends have power too. The power levels vary with the hour of the day and with your diet and your sexual activity. If you have a Significant Other, you can work with that one to increase your power output dramatically. These workings are not weird mystical hoodoos. They are scientifi-

---

[10]Protective amulets are available from Godolphin House, PO Box 297, Hinton, WV 25951, or on the web at www.wicca.org.

cally proven and easy enough to understand. They are fact. It's just that this hidden or occult knowledge has been forbidden to you. With a few moments' effort, you can prove to yourself that what we claim is fact, not fiction or fantasy. Be aware, though, that once you have felt your own natural inborn power, your life will forever change.

May the Force be with you.

CHAPTER TWO

WHY BOTHER?

WHY

You may think of this as the *why* chapter:

Why bother?

Why do you need a ritual?

Which *why* should you select for your first ritual?

The chapter has three sections:

1. Why Bother?
2. Reasons for Ritual
3. Identifying which *why* you will start with.

THE LAST RESORT

Sometimes it seems as though there is no possible solution to a problem. That is when many of us turn to magic. Over the many years that we have been doing magic, we have learned that magic follows certain rules, and that if a practitioner follows those rules in the expectation that circumstances will change, then circumstances *will* in fact change. Often it seems that a situation must be at its blackest and all mundane avenues must be explored and exhausted before people will attempt even the most simple ritual. Many of us in the alternative world, too, dislike asking for help. So this book is designed as a self-help manual that will equip you to construct your own rituals and make sure that you complete all the essential steps.

In the time when people were first working with electric power, many individuals were injured and even killed—in all innocence—because the laws of electricity were not yet fully understood. Today people understand pretty well how electricity works and how to use it sensibly and safely. You would not stick your finger into a socket, because you know better. If you are new to magic, learn the rules of its working. Be sensible and safe. You need not reinvent the wheel yourself; that's been done.

This book recommends only rituals that are *safe*, *ethical*, and *effective*. Remember this fact with the acronym built on the initials of those adjectives:

SEE.

First Things First

It is of prime importance to decide what the ritual will be *for*. Why go to all the trouble, after all, if you can't articulate a reason for it?

Most ritual workings are for money, companionship, and health.

So you're short of money. How bad is the situation in the real world? Are you actually hungry and facing a bare cupboard—or is it just that you can't go to that upscale restaurant tonight? Are creditors calling every day? Did the car break down yet again and the mechanic warn you that it can no longer be healed because the body is more rust than metal—or is it that you'd just like a brand-new SUV with all the glitz and glitter you can pile on it? Remember that lowering your expectations and not lusting after the latest fad electronic toy, flashy car, sex symbol, or whatever saves you just as much money as, if not more than, working more hours. Adjusting your expectations to fit reality is just as important as plumping up your income.

Maybe you are lonely or sexually deprived. You'd better decide which it is before you start planning the ritual solution to your discomfort. How urgent is the problem? So you want a more attractive companion. Are you sure you aren't being tempted by the images you see on TV or in skin magazines?

Health is probably an easier subject to assess. If you or someone close is ill, and has explored all the mundane channels, but is getting even sicker, then you can figure out how urgent the necessity of healing really is.

Let's be really honest. Fill in the chart that is Work Sheet II-1. Its left-hand side says "Present Situation." Its right-hand side says "What I Want." Once you've done that, you can go through and identify your most urgent needs, then fill in the Effort column. Decide how much effort you are willing to put into fulfilling any given need. Are you willing to spend four or five hours a day for a couple of weeks preparing for a ritual? In other words, how much of you are you willing to put on the line for this thing that you've decided is a necessity?

When you have decided how many hours you will invest, perhaps you'll feel that you could attain your necessity by mundane means rather than by magical means. Will the result be obtained if you invest the same number of hours in such mundane activities as improving your job performance or taking a course?

When the Effort column is filled out, the Ranking column may be easier to complete. Of course the sequence in which you think about the columns is your own choice. Don't forget that none of these entries is engraved in stone. You can shift and fine-tune them as your perceptions evolve.

As you rank your priorities, be careful to get the order right. Where does *money* come? If you want a more fulfilled life, where does *companionship* come? Which—in your individual circumstances—should come first? What is your most pressing need? Here an old puzzle can serve as a parable.

> A Yukon fur trapper was out on his trap lines when snow began to fall very heavily. As the snow abated, the temperature plummeted. He was lucky to struggle through the deep drifts back to his cabin without freezing to death. Back at the cabin, he discovered he had only one match remaining. In the cabin he had a candle, an oil lamp full of oil, and a fire already laid with kindling (though not lit). Which should he light first? The answer: The match.

In ranking your priorities, don't gallop off in all directions at once. If you are flat broke and want to attract the sexy blonde film-star, the match you light should be money. If, on the other hand, you have a good job with a little money in the bank and a brand-new car, then your match will probably be a companionship ritual. It is not really possible to do two or three rituals all at once. Your result would be a confused mess. One at a time is what you have to do, and therefore you must decide which one to work on first.

Present Situation	What I Want	Effort*	Rank

Work Sheet II-1*
Prioritizing

*Hours. A typical simple ritual will require at least thirty hours to prepare and perform. If you decide on a major multiperson effort, figure that success will depend on a minimum of a hundred hours of real work.

Eddie L Cures Himself

Eddie L was a truck farmer near Topeka, Kansas. In common with other farmers in the area, he routinely used enormous amounts of agricultural chemicals—fertilizers, pesticides, herbicides—the whole arsenal of chemical warfare. Eddie was a very likeable, popular fellow whose hobby was fiddling at the many local fiddle contests. He had won several prizes, and could always be guaranteed to be among the leaders anywhere he went. He had even cut a couple of CDs that sold with moderate success.

One day Eddie woke up already packed and eager to get on the road to his next gig, where he knew he would place among the top three contestants. To his horror he found that the entire right side of his body was paralyzed. He spent many thousands of dollars on tests over the next six months. The medical profession finally gave up on him; they essentially wrote him off as a total loss. So far as anyone could detect, he had somehow drunk or ingested some of his agricultural chemicals, and this had caused permanent nerve damage.

In one of our books Eddie read our mention of Tim Wheater, once flautist with the Eurhythmics. Tim had been a victim of an accident involving agricultural chemicals; the difference was that his entire body was paralyzed, not just one side. Though a medical write-off like Eddie, Tim had traveled to India, had learned to tone, and over time had healed himself with toning.

Eddie learned that Tim would lecture in San Francisco, and with no little difficulty arranged to attend the lecture. It inspired him to set up for himself a morning ritual. Instead of toning he would play one continuous note on his violin, using his paralyzed right hand to hold the bow while his left hand moved the violin against the bow. Holding the bow was very difficult at first, but when he hooked his thumb through it, he managed it. Every morning for fifteen minutes he played that single note. It took almost three months, but eventually his right hand began to respond and he found he could move the bow while he held the violin still. From then on, his little self-designed ritual worked wonders. Somehow the brain must have made new nerve connections so that now, although Eddie's walk still manifests a slight unevenness, he is essentially healed.

The persistence that Eddie showed came from his own high self-confidence. When he read of Wheater's recovery, his immediate reaction was, "I can do that!" So with just fifteen minutes a day in a morning ritual, he did it too.

Eddie's Ritual Plan

Without the knowledge that others had cured themselves, and without his own good opinion of himself, Eddie might never have cured himself. An essential part of his cure was the personal ritual he put together.

Every dawn he got up, faced the sun, and reinforced his self-esteem with the affirmation:

> *I can cure myself.*
> *As I will, so let it be.*
> *I take the energy of the new sun*
> *into myself to aid in this cure.*

Then he would tone an E, to find out what specific pitch or tone his body needed to help it heal on that day.[1] Then looking at a picture of himself receiving one of his many awards, he played that single note on his violin for a full fifteen minutes.

Reasons for Ritual

There are probably as many reasons to do a ritual as there are people in the world. But we can break those reasons down into different types. The majority of people coming to us ask for *secular* or *mundane* rituals. These are procedures to change the future in your own physical world, in such a way as to make it more to your liking. In this category the two most popular are those to bring more wealth into your life, and those to bring companionship. Naturally

---

[1] To do this all you do is tone, to the best of your ability, "eeeeeeeeeeeee." It should sound like *beet* with the *b* and the *t* off the ends. Start very low and deep, and gradually raise the pitch until you go as high as your voice will let you. Breathe at will when you need to. Somewhere in the ee-continuum there will be a break, a tone that you can't do. This is the tone your body needs for healing.

you must define the *intent* of the ritual before you design the ritual itself. For instance, is the companionship you seek for friendship, love, sex, or whatever? Let us look for a moment at typical "needs."

MONEY

Why do you think you want more money? Is it because you're trying to keep up with some artificially high living standard—to have all the shiny toys that all your friends have—or is it that you want to impress your Significant Other? *Why?* Is it envy? An honest answer to that question may remove the need for doing *any* ritual! It's unsettling to think that over 80 percent of the world's population lives on less than $25 a week.

Some friends of ours, Robbie and Bridget, lived in an upscale condominium near Baltimore. Their combined annual income approached $100,000. Because they had all the toys that modern society seems to require, and because they sent their children to private schools, they were still driving two old clunkers that kept breaking down. Their chronic lament was "We need more money!" and if we went to a ritual with them, they routinely complained about having to pay a couple of dollars at the gate. It's simply a matter of priorities. With a more realistic prioritizing, they would have had money to spare for the better cars they genuinely needed, even if they had to cut back on their entertaining and fad purchases.

If you are on welfare and it's running out, maybe you need more money right now, but it turns out that most people don't.

COMPANIONSHIP

As with any other situation, you need to define *why* you want a new companion or more friends. If you are a couch potato living alone and never going out, not even deigning to go to local night spots or singles bars, or take a course in an interesting subject at your city's college, or invite your fellow workers and their families to dinner, you have no social interaction. Even if you run a ritual for companionship, it is unlikely that the ritual will work to fulfill your desire unless you place yourself in positions where you are likely to meet people whom you would like. Have you even looked in the newspaper at the weekly calendar of upcoming events? Answer the question *Why?*, and you will quickly identify the type of ritual you can do to bring about a new, more social life.

We often feel that people in this searching mode do themselves a terrible disservice when they assume that the first thing they need is a new and different companion. Relationships take work, and today's world seems to deny this fact. Too many people feel that:

"I'm entitled to a relationship with total mutual understanding and support from the get-go."

This mysterious way of thinking is often fostered by the Hollywood mythos of the Leave-It-to-Beaver type family. We hope you are adult enough to see through such an artificial world. And we wonder why you feel you are entitled. Were you particularly good in a past life, or what?

It doesn't work that way. Your authors have been married—to *each other*, in fact—for over thirty years, and there are some very rocky patches on that long road. But we both made a large investment in each other. Affection, time, learning curve, a spiritual path that we founded—all these things and more are experiences mutually shared; walking away from it all would simply make no sense. It would be both wasteful and ineffective.

Think long and hard before you dump a five- or ten-year relationship. Once the novelty of the new companion has worn off, once the honeymoon is over, is the sex going to be any better than with the old person? Is the mutual understanding going to be any better? If you answer these questions "Yes," a new-companionship ritual might be in order. Divorce is, after all, an opportunity for new beginnings—a milestone, not a defeat—as well as the completion of a stage in your life (lives). Let's be honest. It may have been a mistake in the first place—an honest decision, but made for the wrong reasons. A certain number of well-meaning young people marry because of their hormone drive, led by their genitalia rather than their head or even their heart, and duped into believing that without marriage there is no sex. Such a marriage may too often lead to disaster. So use your head in evaluating new possible companions and in doing a companionship ritual.

HEALING

Here we think specifically in terms of healing yourself or a very close companion or associate. The question *Why?* asks not why the healing is needed, but instead why the person has the health problem.

"Why do I continually get month-long flu episodes? Why does every passing children's disease seem to latch on to me?" Now you're into a realm that requires a painfully detailed, real-world look at the patient's lifestyle. For in the lifestyle you may find various stress factors that prompt the patient to have the disease to avoid unpleasant reality, or as a bid for sympathy, to get attention, or to avoid some situation like a promotion they're not sure they can handle, or to buy time resisting some unattractive life assignment.

Why, why, why? In this as with all cases, write down several alternative possibilities. Use the tools described below to identify which of the possibilities is the most likely. Once you and the patient have identified probable factors in the illness(es), you can design a ritual or make a change in lifestyle—or do both, of course—to correct the situation and effect the healing.

SERENITY

Why are you not serene? Has your family split up? Are you afraid of a future breakup? Are you afraid your kids aren't safe in school? Do you worry that your sex life is going down the toilet? Are you afraid that people are not being honest with you? Do you feel that there must be more to life than what you have achieved? Are you facing some major life-transition?

Sometimes in helping people we find that when they were children, someone said or did something very negative to them. You know the sort of thing: "She was hit all over with an ugly stick." "He missed the line for brains." "She's the smart one; her sister is the pretty one." Such remarks stay with a person for the rest of their life. Even worse are the remarks of those who would control your whole life. Preachers know only too well how to inflict guilt, shame, and fear from their pulpits. Most of the congregation are used to it and let it wash off, but young children are impressionable and can be scared (or scarred—take your pick) for life. Few people miss qualifying to be numbered among the walking wounded.

We cannot answer for you the often painful question of "Why am I unhappy?" You must do that difficult work for yourself, even if it means tears and months of searching heartache. This is exactly the question that we encourage you to ask yourself in all cases of figuring out the reason for a serenity ritual.

A recurrent clue crops up in people's search for serenity, and it may be your problem too. That is, that many people search *outside* for serenity when they should be looking *inside*. They think something Out There will fill the void they feel.

When the cause is in the distant past, it takes a very powerful, often traumatic, ritual to overcome it. The early program tapes that are in your head have to be erased and replaced. A new and different job, a new and different companion, a healing—none of these will cure the problem forever. This is the underlying reason that many people move on from job to job and companion to companion in an endless search, never fixing the *internal* problem.

PROTECTION

In this day and age, it sounds weird to imagine that someone may have cast the evil eye on you. In fact you may have been hexed by some knowledgeable envious "friend." There are many quite mundane rituals that you can do to overcome such a situation. The question first to be answered is, Why do you think you have been hexed? And why would somebody go to the rather considerable trouble to do it to you? Are you that important? List your possible hexers and use the techniques described below to ascertain which is the most likely candidate. What reason would they have to wish you ill? Once the candidate is identified, you can do some elementary protective rituals to guarantee that anything sent toward you will be returned to the sender.

Ho Hum, or Urgent Necessity?

At the outset you need to understand: The thing that drives ritual is your emotion or the emotion of the group that is doing the work.

Without emotion, the enterprise will fall flat and die without a gasp. If you are in a ho-hum mood that says, "It would be nice to have that, but it isn't an urgent necessity," then it's quite likely that the ritual will accomplish precisely nothing except maybe add to your frustration.

Rituals can serve any purpose. They can be practical—for gaining money, new companionship, healing, and generally improving your life. They can be spiritual—getting you in touch both with your inner self and with other spiritual realms. They can be binding, as when a group does a ritual together to reaffirm their mutual interest and the group's strength. This last type is sometimes called a feel-good ritual. It should make all participants feel glad they share with one another something so important and so beneficial.

In thousands of cases there may seem to be no simple solution to a problem. Here magic will either change your direction or make the problem go away. Typical of this sort of ritual is one you might do when your boss is a real stinker. You might do a ritual to get the boss fired; you might do a ritual to get a new job. Remember, though, that in considering a ritual you need to think through all the effects it will have downstream—the fallout from your work. There is a thing we call the Law of Attraction. If you do a ritual to get someone fired, you may find that the someone is you. Think again about the SEE idea—be sure your ritual is safe, effective, and ethical.

Rituals can be very simple, one-on-one, like the laying-on of hands, or very complex large group workings designed to heal the whole earth. Let's look at a couple of examples.

Jo Cures Eli's Sprained Ankle

Many years ago a well-known Wiccan leader, Eli, visited our home in St. Charles, Missouri. He hobbled in with a leather brace on his ankle. He told us that he had actually torn a ligament and cracked a bone in the ankle. Our daughter Jo, then four years old, said, "I can cure that, just like Mum does." Perhaps just being indulgent, Eli took off the brace and let her hold his ankle between her little hands. In a moment she said, "There. That's done." She picked up the brace and put it tidily into the trash. Eli stood up, put his weight onto the ankle, and found it was in fact completely healed. No big fireworks, no heavy-duty bells and whistles, no great balls of fire. Jo did a very simple laying-on-of-hands ritual, an approach used since before recorded history. Somehow no one had told her young mind that it couldn't be done.

Witches Heal the Earth

At a site in western West Virginia strip miners had been at work doing what is euphemistically called mountain-top removal, to get at coal that lay deep beneath hundreds of feet of soil and rock. The work implies creating a huge hideous scar on the earth and throwing the *overburden* into the nearest watercourse, killing the stream itself and everything in it. The effort had left a mess. The State had come in and put some topsoil back, but very little was growing. In summer, when we were there, it looked like a cross between the Sahara Desert and a bombed-out moonscape.

Every pagan and Wiccan we know longs to own a piece of the Mother, so a large group of Witches, probably two hundred, decided they would buy the site. They had absolute confidence that they could heal the Earth. They bought it for $10 an acre, simply because no one else thought it could be brought back to life.

The group prepared very intensely for the working. Skilled astrologers chose the most favorable hour for the procedure. Tapes of *Music to Grow Plants by* were played over and over, all around the site. All of us who attended wore green robes.

We chanted, drummed, raised power, danced, and made our appeal to the plant devas as we celebrated our life force.

Within two weeks the entire area was green. Looking at the site today, you would never know, save for the contours of the terrain, that it had been a wasteland.

Rituals can be extremely simple with almost no preparation, as Jo's laying-on-hands was, or extremely complex and intense, with lots of work beforehand as the Witches' ritual was. Over the years we have come to believe that the complex rituals work best—those that have a lot of prior thought put into them and are tuned to the purpose at hand. So in this book we will concentrate on the complex approach to ritual, though we hope you will remember that if you have enough self-confidence you can try them without all the preparatory steps. It is certainly better to do *something* than just to sit around and moan about what a rotten hand the Fates have dealt you.

Choosing Where to Put the Magical Energy

You have completed Work Sheet II-1 and decided that money is the key to your present problems. Magically you could do a ritual simply asking for money to manifest in your life and it would undoubtedly work. But (and it's a big But) you might be very unhappy at the way in which it came to you. Someone might die and leave you an inheritance; you might be involved in an accident and get an insurance settlement. There are hundreds of ways in which money can come to you. To avoid unpleasant surprises, it's better to do a focused ritual, one where you specify the source.

There are obviously some very mundane ways of improving the situation—living on beans and Kool-Aid™, getting a second job, getting a promotion, going bankrupt, winning a lottery, selling blood, and countless other approaches. Any of these options will improve your finances. It is up to you to decide which you will consider and do a ritual for. Now look at the list. A ritual isn't needed to, say, sell blood or to go bankrupt or to live on beans and Kool-Aid™. From our limited list, the only three that a ritual would help are to get a second job, or to get a promotion, or to win a lottery. Then you could do a ritual focused on that specific goal. This gives you a ritual for quite specific results, for money from a known source.

"Yes, but—" you may cry, "how do I know that's the best choice?"

There are many ways to ascertain that. We will discuss three very simple techniques.

First list the final most likely options. Number them and come up with a visual image as to what the result of that particular option's fulfillment would be. Fill in the probable consequences (the trade-offs or fallout) of any given action. To skip this essential step is to invite unguessed consequences. Table II-1 gives an example of a completed table. Work Sheet II-2 is a blank for you to use.

Option	Fallout	Item	Vision*
Get a second job	Less free time	1	You in bed tired
Get a promotion	More worry and responsibility	2	You directing people
Win the lottery (BIG)	No problems	3	A blizzard of dollar bills

Table II-1
Example of Options and Visions
*If your perception is not visual, then put in a sound, an odor, or a feeling instead of a vision.

Option	Fallout	Item	Vision*

Work Sheet II-2
Your Options and Visions

Method 1. Make and use a pendulum.

The most elementary tool you can use to decide which of several options to pursue is a pendulum. Take a small card and write on it numbers from one to nine in a small half-circle. Tie a piece of dental floss to a small weight such as a heavy bead or a wheel nut. This forms your pendulum. Carefully hold the pendulum over the card and see to which number it gravitates.

In order to get your conscious mind out of the loop, have a friend renumber the options in your work sheet without telling you the new numbers; then use your pendulum to select a number blind.

Method 2. Dream your way to a solution.

You dreamed last night—whether you remember it or not. You may not remember the dream, but current research shows that everyone dreams. There are two basic reasons why you may not remember your dream.

  1. You were too tired when you went to bed.

When you go to bed really tired, you go into a deep-sleep state. In that state you dream, but the curtain between the conscious and the unconscious is impenetrable.

  2. Unexpected impressions.

Most people dream in pictures; but a finite number dream in the other senses. Instead of pictures, they get impressions as sounds, smells, tastes, and emotion.

To find out which choice you should make, take your copy of Work Sheet II-2 to bed with you. Have a restful night, and dream your dreams. In the morning see whether you remember any dream that had one of the "visions" that you had listed. In most cases this dreaming-with-seed, as we call it, will give you the direction you need to go.

Method 3. Channel a decision.

We recommend that everyone spend fifteen minutes a day channeling. This allows the two halves of your being to re-contact each other and brings serenity into your life. For the present work, we recommend that you make a tape recording of the following guided shamanic journey and play it at a quiet time when you are sure you will not be disturbed. Listen to it and let the mind go free. If you do not have a quiet area, you can get a drumming tape and play it as loudly as possible to cover up background noise.[2] If you

---

[2]A drumming tape is available from Godolphin House, PO Box 297-B, Hinton WV 25951, or on the web at www.wicca.org.

have a drummer friend who will help you, two rhythms are required. Rhythm 1 is a continuous beat. Rhythm 2 is popularly known as the Maxwell House beat. (Ta-ta ta-ta TA ta-ta, ta-ta TA, etc.)

Before you start, review Work Sheet II-2. Expect to bring back one of the "visions" you listed in the work sheet. This time you are channeling with seed. This channeling happens without any sense of haste and without interruption from any source.

To Rhythm 1:

> You are walking along a river bank. It is springtime. The weather is beautiful and the temperature very agreeable. You can smell the pine from the trees you are walking among and hear the birds above the rippling of the river. As you walk along you decide that the path is sandy enough to take your shoes off. Now you feel the coarse sand under your feet. You come to a cliff where the river becomes a waterfall and you stop and feel the spray on your face and listen to the rushing waters. Suddenly in the cliff face you see a door. On the door is a handle that displays a strange design which, although it is strange, fascinates you. Somehow it feels known to you. You decide that this is your special design. You try to remember it. When you put your hand on it, the door opens. It leads into a cave that seems to be lit with its own inner glow. It is a warm light and the cave feels comfortable. You think you hear faint music in the distance, and you certainly smell a pleasant odor. You walk into the cave and it becomes misty. Through the mist an animal comes and welcomes you. You must remember the animal because it is your ally from the animal world. The animal takes your hand and leads you forward. You come to a large open space with a domed ceiling. A staircase spirals up one side of the space. The animal leads you toward the staircase, and you climb it. At its top there is another door. It has the same type of handle as the outer door. As soon as you touch this handle, the door opens. Your animal friend indicates that it will stay and guard the door for you. The room you enter is rather unusual: Every time you think about part of it, it changes to match your thoughts. There is a comfortable couch in the room and as you look at it, it changes, first into a loveseat and then back into a couch; one that you have always liked. You see that the windows are draped, and you change the draperies to those you would enjoy. There is a table in

the room. You adjust the temperature to your liking. You adjust the background music to your liking. You adjust the scent to your liking. In fact you make the room your room. Now you are going to give the room a name—any name you like. It can be simply "My Room." It might be "Safe Place," "The Chamber," or "The Cave," or any name at all.

Change to Rhythm 2:

You lie down on the couch and drift. Your spirit separates from your body. You notice in your spirit form that there is a well in the corner of the room. You go down into the well and feel the enclosing weightlessness of the water. It's at perfect body temperature. In the bottom of the well you see a light, and you drift down through the water to it. When you get there you see it looks like an eye, and you know you're supposed to go through the middle of it. When you go through the eye, you arrive at the bottom of a gently sloping hill covered in flowers. At its top there seems to be some kind of little white marble temple. You know that the temple contains all the answers you need. So you drift across the flowers toward it.

At this point there is no more guidance, but the drumming should continue for about ten minutes. Or there should be a ten-minute blank on the tape. Then the drumming should change back to Rhythm 1. This is a message to bring you back into the "real" world.

It is time to come back. Back down across the field of flowers, back through the eye. Rejoin your body on the couch, and go to the door and walk out of your room. You find yourself immediately back in your body in your living room (or wherever you are).

Take a quiet moment to review what happened. Have a glass of water or wine. Come back into the real world.

Notice that all three of these options require that you complete Work Sheet II-2 with several alternative solutions to the problem you face. We recommend at least four, so the chart allows for five. If your attempts at finding the best track fail after three attempts, that tells you to go back and rethink your options.

Yes, but Bert Wasted Two Weeks and a Thousand Dollars

Bert is a pleasant man who works at our local feed mill in Salem, Missouri. He was troubled by bouts of eczema. Finding no help from his "regular" doctor, he turned to a local herbalist. The herbalist's salve, at half the price of the professional salve, seemed to work quite well in relieving the symptoms of the eczema; but what Bert wanted fixed was the underlying *cause*. That was most probably the fine dust generated by the grain conveyor in the feed mill. He went to a shaman in Rolla, Missouri, who did a long and involved shamanic cleansing ritual for him. The cost to Bert was really nothing beyond a small fistful of dollars and a couple hours of his time. For some weeks he seemed free of eczema. Then he got it again and it seemed worse than ever.

Bert was a member of the Church of Wicca, and he told us his sad story three weeks later. It was clear and simple to us. We told him, "Change jobs."

Bert had all the usual "Yes, buts—"; "Yes, but I'm not skilled at anything else." "Yes, but there are very few other jobs in the small town of Salem." "Yes, but I have a wife and children to feed." "Yes, but I have a lot of seniority at the mill."

"You don't have to leave the mill; just ask to be put on some other job."

"Yes, but I'm the only one who knows all the mixes."

"All right then," we said, "continue using the salve and don't worry about it."

"Yes, but my wife doesn't like me scratching."

"So get some dust-proof clothing." We were not awfully sympathetic because to us magic is to be used respectfully, to solve those problems on which the professionals have given up on or are really very urgent.[3]

Although Bert did not take our advice, he respected our opinion; and so a week later when he heard of a job opening for a deliv-

---

[3]As tax-exempt clergy, we can legally heal only documented members of the Church of Wicca.

ery truck driver, he was back on the doorstep asking for a ritual that would land the job for him. We pointed out that no ritual in the world would get him the job until he had a heavy-goods-vehicle license to drive a truck. We suggested he enroll at a nearby school that taught drivers professional skills.

His response? Another set of "Yes, buts," starting with "Yes, but they want a thousand dollars!" and ending with, "Yes, but I have to take two weeks off."

At that point we told him to make a list similar to Work Sheet II-2 and to dream on it for three nights. None of his "visions" came through. We tried running the pendulum on his options. It didn't respond, so we turned to the tarot. The cards said any change of job would be disastrous. Bert didn't want to believe it. Instead he bit the bullet and took the course and got his HGV license. Once he started driving the delivery truck, he never again showed any signs of eczema.

So what was magical about all that?, you might ask.

Nothing. But Bert effectively healed himself by gaining the understanding that when there is a mundane problem to be solved, it is best to use mundane means. When someone is about to shoot you, your protective amulet is not likely to stop the bullet unless the bullet actually hits it. Your protective ritual must change the mind of the person who is attacking you; or you must mundanely remove the reason for the attack.

About a month later there was a dust explosion in a feed mill in New Bern, North Carolina. A man died. OSHA then started a heavy inspection program. Lo and behold, our local mill in Salem had to make extensive changes, covering open conveyors and installing exhaust fans with filters. The very next week we had a blizzard. Because Bert lived close to the mill, and because delivery trucks could not get through the snow, he worked in the mill mixing feed. No eczema! If he had followed the magical advice, he need not have done anything.

There are, then, two different approaches to solving any problem you may have. One is *mundane* and one is *magical*. "Magical" techniques, such as the pendulum, dreaming, channeling, or whatever means you like, will help you decide which approach to take. In following through on what you learn, you may in fact use mundane techniques such as taking a second job, taking a course, or even selling some of your blood for immediate cash. The *combination* of the mundane with the magical can work wonders in your life. You can truly manifest anything.

What This Chapter Shows You

First, and most important, we have opened with this chapter to offer guidelines on how to determine *why* you want a ritual, and *why* this specific one at this time, and *why* you think no mundane, nonmagical change in your life without benefit of ritual will fit your urgent necessity.

What This Book Shows You

1. The object or goal of the ritual—in other words, why bother?
2. The amount of effort required to accomplish the goal.
3. The supplies and mind keys you will need to obtain.
4. How to complete a flow chart defining every aspect of the work and the sequence of events.
5. How to choose the time when astrological influences will be most favorable.
6. How to determine where you will do the work.
7. Guide you to the need for other participants who may work with you, and show you how to rehearse them.
8. How actually to do the ritual you have planned.
9. Determine how effective your work was in the real world.

CHAPTER THREE

WHAT DO YOU REALLY WANT?

LIVING SOMEONE ELSE'S DREAM?

In the title of this chapter the emphasis is on *you*, not on your spouse, your children, your parent, your teacher, or your boss. Many people in this world get trapped into living lives designed to fulfill their parents' dreams. The doctor's son or daughter becomes a physician. The actor's child goes into show business. This goes on unto the third or fourth generation, no matter the real wishes of the trapped offspring. Now is the time in your life when you need to decide whether the career you are in suits you and what career would suit you better. Have you ever even taken an aptitude test? How on earth do you know what your natural abilities fit you for?

Gavin started out as an engineer because his *father* always wanted to be an engineer but was trapped into the family business. Such a fate is a travesty. Gavin experienced a major life-change in his mid-thirties, with the realization that he would much prefer to be a writer, not an engineer, and that his spiritual beliefs were wildly at variance with those of his wife and his family members.

Once he had gone through that epiphany, he gradually changed his lifestyle. A divorce settlement required him to make certain payments toward alimony and child support; that fact restricted his job possibilities for years. Once the majority of the payments were off his back, he walked away from being an engineer and became a writer and teacher. The transition was painful at times. At one period he had to go on food stamps, in a dramatic comedown from the gold charge cards implied by his earlier executive position. After not having worn a suit and tie for more than thirty years, the pain of the change has dimmed. For his own mental and physical health he *had* to make that transition.

He knew he was in the wrong career. How do you feel about yours?

Lottery Winners Are Losers

Are you hoping that some *deus ex machina* will come and zap! splat!, everything will change? The splat! might be the winning of a lottery, or the love of another companion, or any of a thousand things. And you can in fact help make it happen by doing rituals. But once it has happened, will you be happy? Will you spend the lottery money judiciously? Or will you spend it, as many do, foolishly and frivolously and too quickly? The statistics are almost unimaginable, but the usual lottery winner takes only *two years* to go through a million dollars and be back dependent on his previous job and wage. Twenty-four months.

A friend of ours, whose public name is Dr. Leisure, was a professor of recreation management. An intriguing lecture of his was titled "What Would You Do with a Million Dollars?" The students of whom he asked the question normally came up with rather predictable responses: travel, get out of debt, and, in rare cases, maybe a little charity work. Dr. Leisure would persist. "What after that?"

"More travel, maybe—a new motor home to travel around the United States."

"Then what?"

Not one student ever said, "I'll invest it, retire, and improve the quality of my life."

In fact many people are such poor planners that when they retire, they settle down at the idiot box, vegetate, and die. Research shows that if such retirees do not get into some activity within five years of retiring, their life expectancy is about 72. Shocking? Yes. So before you go out and buy all those lottery tickets and do the ritual to make one of them win, think about it. Plan.

Yes, all those bright, shiny new things seem very attractive— but if nothing else, think about the effect you're having on the ecology of the planet. If you steadily buy new instead of using items to a logical worn-out point, you are just adding to the landfill and to the burdens your children's children will bear. And when you move to that glitzy new mansion in the fashionable end of town, do you want to hire *three* moving vans for your staggering inventory of big-ticket toys?

QUALITY OF LIFE

Instead of thinking about how much more money you need, or how you need to change your present companion, how about thinking from the other end? If I were laid off tomorrow, how much money would it take to keep me and my family alive? And what would I be buying with it? Instead of getting rid of the present Significant Other, how about trying some counseling? What happened to the relationship that started out so fine? Could it be salvaged? Is the present setup so bad that you're willing to spend thousands upon thousands of dollars to change it? And why do you think a new relationship won't degrade in the same way?

Aren't we all looking for a better quality of life? If you really enjoy your work, then a few extra hours of overtime might be the way to go; but most of us are pretty glad to get away from it and relax.

Your authors are well past the conventional retirement age, and there aren't hours enough in the day to do all the things we want to do. We have projects and plans ahead of us that we may never get to. Sitting on our shelves now are stacks of Spanish learning tapes that we haven't opened. A couple of years ago, French learning tapes occupied that spot. Those tapes opened up so many things to do and places to explore that we know now our lives will not be long enough to do them all.

What do you look forward to? Just more of the same old grind—or a light at the end of the tunnel, when debts will be paid off and you can work less and play more? What's around the corner for you? How can you improve the quality of your life?

Feng shui (the Chinese art of placement) teaches that if you have a dominant electronics corner in the room, you should cover that corner with a heavy blanket or even a piece of carpet fabric. That will cut down the electronic time wasters in your life. Granted, some television programs have a great deal of valuable information to offer, and some lift you up because they are really humorous. And some release you because they take you through an emotional catharsis. We are not saying dump all TV programs; nor are we saying dump all your Internet excursions. What we *are* saying is, use some judgment and try to decide what wastes time that would be better spent improving the quality of your life socializing with other humans—or doing as we do, going ballroom dancing. We hear the outburst of "Yes, buts." In this book, though, you are not allowed any "Yes, buts." You are allowed only the "Yeses."

Now is the time to complete the Quality of Life chart, Work Sheet III-1. In the first section, enter how many hours you spend each week in the activities listed. Then list the number you would *like* to spend in the activity. Notice that *work* and *housework* are two separate entries, and that *housework* should include cooking meals.

Activity	Hours per week	
	Present	**Desired**
Work: Basic hours		
- Overtime (enter second job here)		
- Housework		
Sleep		
Sex: Basic		
- Romance		
Eating: Sustenance meals		
- Pleasure meals		
Hobbies		
Entertainment: Movies		
- TV: Time-wasting		
- TV: Real entertainment		
- TV: Educational		
- Live shows including night clubs or bars		
Computer (hours outside work)		
Exercise: Machine		
- Jogging		
- Dancing		
- Swimming		
Driving: Work- and errand-related		
- Pleasure		
Talking: To Significant Other		
- To children		
Other		

Work Sheet III-1
Assessing the Quality of Your Life

TV, reading, and *computer* are all fairly straightforward, but *sex* may be another matter. In this time, include the amount of time spent in romance—the long hot baths together, the petting times—that is why *romance* is a separate item. If *romance* is at zero, even if sex is up in the region of one hour per day, you are in trouble; because *romance* includes all that person-to-person communication essential for a good long-term relationship.

Edwina and Her Range Rover

Edwina P is a nurse who lived in a small house in a suburb of Chicago, Illinois. She worked downtown in the maternity ward of a hospital that served mostly inner-city poor people. She decided she must have a Range Rover to make sure that, no matter what the weather in the Windy City, she could always get to work and respond to her emergency calls.

The Range Rover is a very expensive piece of British machinery, and Edwina's budget really didn't stretch to it. She performed a ritual to get a better position and a higher salary so that she could afford her Rover. The ritual was very successful. She was offered a supervisory post in a hospital where one of her friends worked in Tampa, Florida. With her very first paycheck in Tampa, she bought her Rover. It didn't matter, of course, that she now had no earthly use for the expensive machine she would be driving. Florida seldom experiences blizzards. Nor had she any intention of ever going off-road—but she had her dream, that Range Rover. The costs and upkeep of the vehicle kept her constantly impoverished, but it was her pride and joy.

The hospital administrator received an offer of a post in Tanzania. He offered to buy Edwina's Rover from her with the idea of taking it with him. She refused to sell, but in discussing his new post with him, she asked about opportunities for American nurses out there. He invited her to work as his assistant. Today Edwina is happy. She has her Rover in Africa. . . .

There's Nowt So Queer as Folks

How much do you pay for a dream? How tightly should you get locked onto the ineffable fantasy? If it makes you happy, then no matter how impractical it is, do it.[1] You work hard; you deserve the rewards you earn. What started out for Edwina as a dream with a very practical consideration of snow and bad weather in Chicago turned itself into an inescapable desire: driving a Range Rover—and who is to say? If she hadn't gotten her Range Rover in this incarnation, she might have had to reincarnate and get it in the next lifetime.

New cars are an essential part of the American dream. The automotive industry knows this only too well and continues to sugar-coat the sell by adding things such as side airbags "for your protection" and selling tall SUVs so that Johnny can see out through that window next to his car seat. "If you're a good parent who cares about your child's education, you'll buy this enormously expensive gas-guzzling whale so Johnny can see the world outside. Don't abuse your child. Buy our SUV." These are the little nudges that get people into the salesroom, to walk out with a new car on an ever-longer payment schedule.

Recently we ourselves traded our old car for a new one because in its rear compartment the new car can carry a printing press. Of course for far less money we could have rented a truck every time we needed to carry the press to its hospital—once or twice a year. But the subtle nudges grew into a new car with a five-year payment schedule. If you are hard up financially, you need to be extra careful about those very subtle nudges. How bad is it really that little Johnny can't see over the ledge of the window? How many hours a day does he spend staring at the upholstery on the car door? It will make him a juvenile delinquent? Does he assume embryo position when he can't see out for those ten minutes? Is he withdrawn and wistful about seeing out, or is he fighting with siblings?

---

[1] Never mind family and friends and their remarks. They are living their lives without your unwanted advice; and until they pay your bills, you are entitled to live your life without *their* advice. Your right? Nay, it is your duty.

Why not be honest and simply admit you want a new car? How old will Johnny be when you pay it off? Some people aren't happy unless they have the most attractive house on the block and that block is in an upscale part of town. We, on the other hand, like to do restorations; the thought of a brand-new house with everything exactly "right" doesn't fit our fix-up-and-salvage-and-recycle approach to life. Many years ago we moved to St. Louis, Missouri, so Gavin could take an executive position in aerospace. The firm had arranged for a specialist in executive relocations to show us local houses. She had gotten the impression "Here is an ideal opportunity for you, a new junior executive moving in, and he needs a home." She showed us houses *starting* in a price range of well over $150,000—and this was over thirty years ago! Today $400,000 probably wouldn't touch them.

We told her "No, no, no, no, no! Help us find a fixer-upper, something under $20,000—close to the plant—something we can afford." That didn't compute with her. Executives had to live in upscale suburbs like Webster Grove, not close to the plant in Florissant. We persisted. She found a wonderful old house with pocket doors and mature landscaping for $18,000 and some odd dollars. It dated from the World's Fair of 1904. Yes, it needed paint and wallpaper. Yes, it needed a new kitchen. But that's what we like to do. Today people call it "sweat equity." It was a wonderful house; it was close to the plant where we could entertain visiting groups, perfect for us and our lifestyle, if a little large—and it didn't consume half Gavin's salary.

We are not suggesting here that you suddenly realize sweat equity is something you've always wanted to do. We *are* suggesting that you and your family can be happy without it costing the earth. There's an emotional price to pay for "better" positions, and the commitment would inevitably imply more hours of work and less quality time with the family.

Our daughter Jo was a single mother on a fast track, managing a Montgomery Ward store (while Ward's was still in business). She worked extremely long hours making a very high salary with almost no time for the baby. We suggested she join us and take over management of the School of Wicca—at a fraction of her salary, but with much improved free time and her own house. The decision was a tough one, but the result has been that she has time for her son and for other civic and social activities. She had to ask in meditation for several consecutive nights before she decided to give up her fast-track career.

The other day we listened to a lecture given by the registrar of Marshall University in Huntington, West Virginia. She made an interesting point. Until very recently, students demanded courses that would lead to high-paying careers in health, computer sciences, or law; and they always wanted to specialize in areas that paid the highest possible money. She has detected a significant move away from that overriding interest in money, toward the reality of life. Students now want careers that feed their interests as well as those that pay reasonably comfortably. They are no longer going flat out for big money; quality of life is "in."

If you are at a point in your life where something needs to change—whether companionship, career, location, or whatever—think about the total change you want, not just the immediate area that hurts the most. Think, "Whither?" There's no point in exchanging a career at one donut shop for a career at another donut shop if what you really want to do is be a missionary in darkest Africa or a poet in Taos, New Mexico.

There are two books we hope you will read before you design rituals to correct your life situation.[2] Then Work Sheet III-1 should help you make these choices. You may need to complete it in the bathroom or in some other private spot because loved ones may not be immediately supportive of your wishes. Change is frightening. Gavin found that out the hard way when he told his first wife that his dream was to go to Oregon and write. Her response was essen-

---

[2]M. Sinetar, *Do What You Love—the Money Will Follow* (Paulist Press). Richard Bolles, *What Color Is Your Parachute?* (Ten-Speed Press).

tially, "And give up all this?" His reply, "That's right," was not acceptable.

Where Will You Be in a Decade?

You are looking here ten years into the future. That may seem like a long time, but relationships can change beyond all recognition; kids grow; businesses fail and other businesses thrive. The shakeout of 2000 and 2001 in the high-tech and dot-com industries showed how difficult and dangerous it is to rely on apparently healthy, growing enterprises. It is often said that employees are more loyal to a company than is the company to its workers. Don't get trapped into the idea that the company is going to go on forever or that your job with the multinational giant is secure. Layoffs are at an all-time high. The very least you should do with the tools from Chapter One is to check and see whether your firm will be in business in ten years' time.

LOCATION
Look now at Work Sheet III-2. Let's start with *Location*. There is an apocryphal story about the German knife manufacturer thinking about opening a factory in the United States. He asked a couple of wealthy American friends, "Where do you go for vacations?"

"Asheville, North Carolina."

So that's where he put the new plant. Have you always yearned to live in the desert? Or Oregon? Or Alaska? Or Hawaii? Have you traveled to the place of your dreams, even for a day or two, to have a real-world glimpse of it? What on earth is stopping you? At our age and semi-retired, we often think about relocating to Europe, to some nation where medical care and prescription drugs are free, where more culture is easily available, where there is good public transportation. Maybe somewhere the baker delivers fresh croissants daily. But when we add up pros and cons, the States always wins— the cost of living in the States is significantly lower than anywhere else. Clearly, though, as we age, the equation will change. Will there be a crossover point? Will we move? Our psychic tools say "Yes," so we keep our options open.

So should you. Enter in the work sheet the place you would most like to live. Then enter when you next plan to visit that area.

Present Situation	Desire	Visit/ Investigate	Realistic Ten-Year Plan
Location			
Housing			
Companion			
Career			

Work Sheet III-2
Your Ten-Year Plan

HOUSING

So you live in an apartment in an area you don't like. You'd rather live in a house out in the woods. Many people feel that they would rather live away from town, and there are lots of positives and negatives to that decision. Not the least is the commute to and from work. If you live in a big city, maybe a small town *would* be a better choice for you. Twenty years ago every pagan in the nation wanted to live in a survival community or an intentional community out in the backwoods. Many did, and many succeeded; but for every one who did succeed, there were ten who found that country living was hard work and subsistence farming was less than a joyous occupation. We have a friend who dreams of log cabins; whether the cabins come from a past-life experience, or whether they are in his future, we cannot determine. Maybe it doesn't matter. The pendulum persistently answers, "Both." So he is looking at the ways and means of building a modern log cabin; and between environmental restrictions and the ever-increasing cost of land, he's finding that it is not the easiest thing in the world to do.

In ten years' time, how many bedrooms will you need? How many square feet of living space? How many garage or other parking slots? And while you are at it, you might as well put down the style of house you would like. Yvonne dreams of an arts-and-crafts bungalow. Gavin really has no preferences in exterior design or style, but wants a dark-beamed dining room. Such little dreams when they come true lead to happiness and contentment. We do live in a cottage; maybe one day we'll put a craftsman-style porch on it. We do have a dining room; maybe one day we'll install faux beams and red flocked wallpaper. Or maybe we'll move. Right now the projects aren't high enough on our priority list even to use the tools at our disposal to find out.

In the Visit/Investigate column enter the approximate date when you will next visit a major home show. There will be at least one a year near you, so no excuses.

COMPANIONSHIP

Chapter Eight contains a set of guides for doing a ritual for a new companion. What we want you to do here is decide what sort of companion you want in your life in ten years' time. Do you want a single companion? Do you want to be part of an extended family? When you are ten years older than you are today, how much of your own autonomy will you release for the others you envision having in your life?

The question is: What do *you* want in *your* future? How many friends? Are you gregarious or are you essentially a loner? Are you sure you know? Many people are surprised when they get a reading from a favorite occultist to learn that in the future they will be part of a large group. Or vice versa—be alone. Write down the alternatives. Use your pendulum or meditative techniques. Write down the answer it gives you. Follow its advice. Remember Eddie?

CAREER

In completing this area, decide how much time you can invest in fitting yourself for your new career. Of course you may be perfectly content and fulfilled in your present career; so skip it. Or if you are not content, you may just want a promotion. In that case, you need to take some business management courses. If you want a career in an entirely different field, you need to figure out how to fit yourself for that. If you want to write novels, for instance, it would be sensible to take a novel-writing course. Here again, enter a specific date when you will start moving toward your new career.

None of that is difficult to understand or plot out.

Now that you have a good idea of where you want to go, start your journey. Plan (and, where necessary, use rituals) to manifest that situation for yourself.

GREG AND HIS JOURNEY

Greg K lived in Erie, Pennsylvania, and was a successful computer programmer. We met him when he attended one of our lectures on meditation and astral travel at the Brushwood Folklore Center in Sherman, New York. The Center regularly runs psychic alternative-spirituality events. Many people go just to camp and get regrounded. The reason Greg attended our lecture? He was at one of those crossroad situations that we all get into. He had an offer from an oil company to go to Saudi Arabia and an offer from an electronics company near San Francisco. During that lecture we did a standard talk-out like the one you can do for yourself from Chapter One.

We didn't really expect that Greg, a novice, would get any dramatic results—but he did. The first surprise was that his animal ally was actually two animals: one a friendly grass snake, the other a venomous cobra. When he got to the talk-out's chamber he found two paths or stairways. He elected to go up the one that the grass snake led him to. He entered the room and he adjusted it, but on a table he noticed articles that had a very oriental look, like old oriental silver. When he went through the eye he found himself in a desert scene; though at first he was afraid, the desert seemed very friendly, not overly hot or threatening. Then the desert scene changed to an area he recognized as San Francisco Bay with Alcatraz at its center; he was in a cell in Alcatraz with the cobra. This frightened him so that he immediately got out of his journey, snapping back into his body.

The interpretation seemed quite clear to us: that he was intended to go to Saudi Arabia.

Any time you find a venomous snake in a journey or in meditation, it indicates something to be avoided. And the idea of being in a prison cell with a cobra reinforced the idea in our mind that was not the place he should go.

Greg followed the path that his journey indicated. At last report he was extremely pleased with his Saudi Arabian job.

"Longest Journey Starts with Single Step"

There are many steps in deciding what ritual is appropriate for you at this time in your life. Completion of the simple work sheets should go fairly quickly. They will help you identify more clearly what may be uncomfortable in your present life, and what you would like your future life to be like. They will suggest a general idea of the steps you'll need to take to get there.

Every ritual—whether mundane, spiritual, or just one to recognize and be grateful for the seasons of the year—should have a beginning, an ending, and a very definite middle. In the middle, the worker(s) clearly states the purpose of the ritual. That statement of purpose should be expressed in the shortest, clearest telegraphic style you can manage. Many ritualists demand that it be reduced to one or two words so that it can be yelled as some other action takes place, such as the clapping-out of a candle. If you do not fill in the work sheets and you do not design your ritual around a real need, it will be very difficult for you to crystallize the ritual's purpose. So get your pencil and start right now defining, analyzing, pruning. Nothing will happen until you do.

Affirmations and Questions

At the heart of every effective ritual is an affirmation or a question. These must be short and succinct. Some long phrase like, "Please help Aunt Edna as soon as you can with her ankylosing spondylitis, if you don't mind" is very difficult to yell out at the top of your voice in the middle of a ritual. It is much better simply to say, "Heal Aunt Edna!" or even "Heal Edna!"

Let's take apart a typical need.

I want a house in Taos
with three bedrooms
on a 5-acre lot
close to town and schools.

1. Delete "I want." If you do a ritual for "I want," you will end up always Wanting, never Getting. If you affirm "I want House X," for instance, in ten years' time you will *still* want House X. Anyhow, the spirits already know you *want* House X. Instead, a simple yell of "House X!" is much more likely to get you the target house.

2. Use a picture of the type of house you would like. The sample affirmation leaves this open. Using the spoken word alone, you could get an adobe, a broken-down clapboard, or a stone, or . . . well, the affirmation is open-ended. The picture will be much more specific.

3. Get a map and visit likely sites. "Close to town" and some of the rest of it might be in the drug lords' area or in the country-club area or in a cluster of muffler shops . . . who knows? Your stipulation should also define the landscape of the lot: Do you want to live in the desert, or on a leafy street, or what?

With the map and the picture in front of you the affirmation becomes "House" or perhaps "Affordable House."

Now think for a moment about the questions you might ask of the pendulum or in a shamanic journey. The answers you get reek of logic. Suppose that on a beautiful hot dry spring day, you ask, "Is it raining outside?" The answer will always be "Yes," because somewhere in the world rain is falling. "Will I get a new job?," "Will I get a promotion?" Two more yeses—but can you do the job well enough to outlast probation? When will the promotion come? Will either change improve your circumstances? Will they make you happier?

Write out in full *exactly* what you want or what your question really is. Be very careful to express this in a form that will bring to you the item or the answer you want.

Then refine it, substituting pictures and maps for long wordy descriptions. Write it as though you were sending an e-mail and each word would cost you $1,000. The old occultists believed that writing it in your own blood was the best way of reducing unnecessary verbiage; you might try that approach.

How Jerry the Trained Occultist Screwed Up

Jerry S. lives in New York City. He got involved with a group of kabalists. He scrupulously learned the mystic meaning of all the paths in the Tree and all the Hebrew names for the various Lights. He could climb the Tree in his head without having even to think about it.

One day he decided to do a ritual for companionship. Of course he did the invocation in Hebrew. Mindful of limiting the number of words, he got it down to one. He was looking for a loving female companion. Instead he got a veritable tartar—a battleship on wheels. He simply used the wrong word.

If your native language is English, use plain modern English. Even English words have changed over the years, but it is the relatively recent meanings that the spirits understand. Don't go self-consciously archaic because you think it makes your cape-swishing more gaspy. Free your work and your thinking of what some people aptly call *god-wottery*. After all, the spirits didn't "pass on" all that long time ago.

Jerry screwed up because

1. He didn't really understand the implications of the Hebrew word, and
2. His pronunciation was off.

Don't fall into that trap. Use whatever is comfortable and natural and clear.

Thus the guidelines boil down to these:

1. Use plain language.
2. Be specific.
3. Clarify and simplify your intent or question.

Others before you have worked in this field. Learn from their mistakes and their successes. You need not reinvent the wheel or chase up blind alleys that are well signposted.

CHAPTER FOUR

How Much Power Do You Need?

In correspondence courses conducted through the School of Wicca, we encourage students to develop their inborn telepathic ability. A good way to do that is to try to influence the dreams of a friend or Significant Other. We suggest they send the image of red roses. Students report success in about 80 percent of attempts.

Katya's Dream Works

Katya W was a student living in Poland. She decided she would try the red-roses exercise but did it with a difference. You should know that she was a very attractive young woman. Indeed, three suitors had asked her to marry. So following our instructions, she got a red rose. At 1 a.m., when she thought her friends would be sleeping, she took the rose and held it, inhaling its very essence, feeling the silky texture of its petals, smelling its classic rose scent, looking deep into its redness, sending these impressions to each suitor in turn. Then she did the same thing half an hour later, and after another half hour she repeated her ritual.

Over the next few days she questioned her friends about their dreams. One said, "I had a very peculiar dream. I was surrounded by a bunch of roses that held me prisoner and finally put me into a jail cell. They were beautiful red roses, and I thought it very odd that they would act like the police."

Another said, "I had a wonderful trip on a cruise boat on the Baltic, going up to see the midnight sun. You were with me. We shared a cabin, and the bed was all made of red roses. Everywhere we went on the ship, there were red roses. They were at our table. You wore one at the final ball."

Her third suitor said, "Yes, roses. I don't know why but I had a dream about them. I was digging them up and making compost of them. It was very, very powerful compost, and it made my garden grow better than ever before. So I went around the neighborhood and stole every red rose I could to make more compost."

Katya thought that the dreams showed the character of each friend to perfection. She married the romantic one with his cruise ship rather than the more practical one with his compost. Of course she dumped the one who regarded them as a prelude to prison. He was definitely a non-starter.

Katya's relationship did not last. She wrote us ruefully, "Romance doesn't put food on the table. I should have chosen the composter."

Targeting

Student experiments and Katya's experience clearly show that one person can affect the dreams of another. In other words, they can telepathically communicate. Katya got very involved with the rose and had a genuine emotional involvement in the outcome of her experiment. Her little ritual worked, even if she made the "wrong" final choice. Thus we are convinced that one person can affect another.

Let's say now that you are involved in trying to stop the earth movers from slashing off another beautiful mountaintop in search of coal. It's very unlikely that you will change the mind of the man driving the heavy equipment if you try it on the day he's actually moving earth. He's involved in his task. He's wide awake and not open to the subtle suggestions that you could give him in the middle of the night when he's asleep. If you had the power of Uri Geller and could bend metal with your mind, then you might be able to damage the fuel system of his machine and buy some time; though you'd be unlikely to stop the rape forever. The only way in these cases is to move up the line and affect the minds of both middle and upper management. Of course those minds are rock-hard set in concrete on the rapacious path they are traveling; so this effort will call for more power than a simple one-on-one.

Since you are dealing with set-in-concrete rapers of the earth, you may be better affecting the minds of a large number of people who will then form a voter bloc wielding enough impact on politicians to change the law.

·Optimal Use of Power

Target	0–100 miles	100–1000 miles	1000–3000 miles*
Sleeping person	1	2	6
Awake person doing repetitive task	2	6	☹
Awake person doing interesting task	6	☹	
Person channeling	1	2	6
Busy executive	☹		
Damage a fuel supply pipe	2	6	☹
Foul up ROM computer memory	1	2	6
Foul up a computer hard drive	6	☹	

Table IV-1
Typical Power Needs for a Successful Ritual

*Land miles. If the target is across water, use the rule of thumb that you must halve the "water" miles; that is, 2,000 land miles equal 1,000 water miles.

☹ = Possibility of success very low, even with very large tuned group.

Table IV-1 will help you figure out the amount of power you need to affect several different types of target at various ranges. Use it as a guide, not a hard-and-fast law unto itself. One night, though, your group may be particularly high and achieve a healing sent from the United States to Europe. On the other hand, a group of six on a low night might not be able to heal someone in the nearest hospital. The table is just a general guide that we've put together from our extensive experience.

Distance Makes a Difference

As Table IV-1 indicates, the energy does dissipate with distance.[1] Russian research has shown that it can be detected up to three thousand miles; and some hush-hush experiments in the American space program have shown that it can be detected even at much greater distances. There are some experiments using mother rabbits and their bunnies, done with submarines. They show that a mother rabbit can detect the energy when one of her young is killed, even when the mother is deep below the central Atlantic in a metal submarine and the baby is two thousand miles away in a laboratory.

We don't know why our results do not more closely parallel those experiments. Perhaps the telepathic message we are sending requires more energy to get through to a human than does the telepathic "noise" of a baby rabbit's death spasm. Maybe human brains are so full of white noise that they cannot clearly receive telepathic information.

The long-range space results suggest that the energy dissipates less in space than across land. Our results across water indicate that energy sent across water dissipates more quickly than energy otherwise directed.

We suggest, "Do not attempt a ritual at over three thousand land miles, and don't ever attempt a ritual that must cross more than one thousand five hundred miles of water." These are very subjective rules, and you may have great success at longer distances. Don't

---

[1]Ostrander and Schroeder, *Psychic Discoveries Behind the Iron Curtain* (Prentice Hall, 1970).

blame us if your long-range ritual seems not to work. Blame the distance instead.

Some workers subscribe to a theory of wormholes in space. They visualize the energy traveling through the interstices of matter and arriving even at long distances with the same power at which it was put out. All we can say is: More experiments in this area need to be done.

Don't waste energy and cause group frustration by picking targets beyond your reach, especially in the early months and years of your work.

Mona and the Bishop

Mona L runs a women's clinic in the deep South. She had been having the usual problems that all women's clinics have in the south: for many months a local fundamentalist church had continually picketed the site. Mona decided to see whether she could magically influence the people who were picketing. She quietly got the names and addresses of the specific members who were most active. She arranged for the clinic's security service to take photographs of the picketers. After a great deal of work she was able to put names to the photographs. She began a nightly ritual of trying to influence the picketers one by one toward her view—not necessarily to make them actively pro-choice, but to get them to lighten up and cut her some slack. She noticed a lessening of the number of people in the picket lines. Try as she might, with some of them she couldn't succeed in getting her message of love and sympathy through. She worked psychically to convert them to her way of thinking by showing them that their hateful attitudes attracted hate to them, that instead they should try to love her patients and bring understanding and pity.

One of the particularly noisy picketers, it turned out, was from out of town, a bishop in the leadership of the church. Mona finally got a group of her friends together to work on the bishop's head. There was no perceptible change. Regularly as clockwork, he would be there on Monday mornings, when traffic at the clinic was highest—even though he actually lived more than five hundred miles away in Tampa, Florida.

We told Mona that she might have more success if she could get closer to the bishop's residence when she did her ritual. We pointed out that from her location the energy had to travel across a large stretch of the Gulf of Mexico and for some reason energy seemed to be absorbed by large bodies of water.

The next weekend Mona and her group traveled to Tampa and did their ritual. The next Monday the bishop was right there on the picket lines again—but he seemed much quieter than before. At noon, when her traffic slowed down, he asked to see Mona.

She was a little concerned at first, especially when he said, "You are the woman I've been dreaming about. Can we talk?"

Talk they did. Mona reviewed several of her appalling case histories with him. She had treated two sisters, 12 and 14 years old, whose father had repeatedly raped them both in particularly vicious ways. Mona showed him actual histories of several similar cases. The bishop reluctantly admitted that in these cases perhaps her work was worthwhile. It was especially disturbing to him that the sisters were members of the congregation in the local branch of his church. He was very concerned when he saw that one of the girls had had two abortions, and had attempted suicide.

He realized that his own congregation had swept things under the rug and had hidden facts that he needed to know. He asked Mona how many other women from the congregation had visited her. She didn't really know the answer to that question: It was only by luck that the bishop had recognized the pictures and names of the two sisters. "If you trust me enough," Mona told him, "and you'll give me the names of your parishioners in this area, I'll look at my files and do a count for you without revealing the names—but you'll have to trust me."

Amazingly the bishop agreed. He learned that more than twenty women in his congregations had visited the clinic; he was smart enough to realize that he needed to fix the problem at its source, not try to forbid those unhappy women their right to Mona's healing. Going against his synod, he stopped the picketing and made several presentations to the synod on the concept of casting the mote out of their own eye before criticizing others.

TARGET TIMING

Chapter Seven talks about maximizing your output of energy and tuning it to the best astrological time for the intent of the ritual. Here, though, you need to consider timing your ritual to the target person's likely activity. When you work to influence an inanimate object like a fuel pipe, of course none of the following is relevant. Most rituals are designed to influence people, though, even if that influence is aimed to work on someone that you will never meet, persuading them to write you that unexpected check.

Your aim: to send the energy toward the target at the best possible time. In our mountaintop mining example, we mentioned that trying to stop the machinery by getting to the head of the man operating it probably won't work. There are two reasons for this:

1. He is tightly concentrating on his job.
2. He's not on a policy-making level anyway.

If you have only a specific time available to do your work, aim at the mind that is more likely to be drifting in those moments. If you can choose the time when you work, aim at the mind of the person who wields more horsepower.

Getting to the boss of the earth-moving man might be easier. Even if he's doing some boring book work, at least he's on a policy-making level; and if he's doing a dull, routine task, getting to his head may be easier than to the head of the one tightly concentrating.

Think again of what you read in Chapter One, The Classic Experiment. From that information you already have a head start on the next level, working on a more distant target.

As Table IV-1 shows, the best time for influencing people is when they are asleep or meditating. Figuring out when they are meditating may be difficult, so we recommend you limit your working to the sleep zone. In general, therefore, we find the best time to transmit telepathic messages is about 1 a.m.

Your success depends on the *sleep state* of the target. Researchers have learned that people regularly and predictably go through different states in dreaming—different levels of involvement. They fall asleep and go into what is called A-state dreaming.

After about ninety minutes there is a period of REM state for about ten minutes. In REM (rapid eye movement) the sleeper is extremely involved in the dream. When your target is in that state, your telepathic message may not penetrate. Thus if you do two rituals about one hour apart, say at 1 a.m. and 2 a.m., you will enormously increase your chances of success. Katya did three consecutive rituals and got excellent results.

Of course this all depends on the lifestyle of the target. If they regularly work third shift or play in a band at a late-night club, then toward dawn might be a better time. It should not be too difficult to find out when the target is likely to go to bed.

Now for each target person, fill in Work Sheet IV-1 to establish the best times for your ritual.

For reasons as yet unknown, but related to the resonance of the Earth's magnetic field, it turns out that working when the sun is below the horizon always gives better results than otherwise.

Target Person	Likely Bedtime	Time for First Ritual	Time for Second Ritual	Distance from Target	Number of Workers

Work Sheet IV-1
Your Guide to Power and Timing

ALICIA'S SPELL FINALLY WORKED

Alicia V lived in Edmonton, Alberta, Canada. She is one of those very happy people, always smiling and up; yet withal she is serious. She had a serious intent to change the attitude of the Alberta government to sled dogs. She believed that more and better laws should be on the books to prevent the abuse and the misuse of these semi-wild huskies. Alicia planned and carried out several rituals. Although she had some success, she fell short of her hopes. When she wrote to us lamenting her problems, we could see nothing wrong in her ritual plan or timing—or for that matter, in the targets she had selected. All were people who would be likely to form a pressure group to get her legislation passed. The people she was trying to influence at first were mainly serious academics. The one thing we could suggest was that she was sending out energy of a type that would not get through to the academics. We told her to change her attitude to the ritual and to try to retune herself just before she did it. Finally things began to start working for her, and today Canadian sled dogs have a much happier life than they had heretofore.

Tune Your Psychic Radio

To tune her psychic radio to a specific intent, a Witch uses a system employing *mind keys*. The system depends on thinking of the various frequencies of the Force as colors, sounds, aromas, feelings, and emotions. Written records dating back as far as two millennia reveal the systems that various magical workers have used to tune the Force for various intents. In groundbreaking work, Yvonne cross-correlated those old sources and constructed a *table of correspondences*. (In Appendix One you will find typical tables.)

Such tables are of inestimable value to the capable Witch; yet paradoxically, you should not take them as absolute gospel for your work. They are only a guide. The keys that *you* feel are appropriate for wealth may not be the traditional keys—and what is more, they may change from day to day depending on your wealth associations and on your mood. Let us say that you associate red with the curing of a blood disease. You might associate red with Valentine's Day, or with the red roses of true love. Yet if you look at a traditional table, true love is associated with Venus and green. Therefore you should sit down and quietly meditate before you do a spell, to decide exactly what mind keys will best tune you to *your* desired frequency.

Almost all occultists and alternative workers use color as their major tuning device, for two reasons:

1. They can see the auric life field around a person and it appears in color.
2. Colors are intimately connected with thought patterns (for example, red = anger or blood; blue = coldness; etc.)

It may be useful to get one of those boxes of children's crayons, one that contains a wide range of colors. Simply selecting the appropriate crayon and coloring a piece of paper with it is enough to give you a basic tuning. Then for reinforcement you can add the other mind keys, from the traditional tables of correspondences or from the keys that work best for you.

As you move through this book, you will be developing mind keys for your own intents and use. You can use the traditional keys as a guide, but you should never lose sight of the fact that *different* keys may be meaningful to you in today's world. A typical traditional color healing chart appears in Appendix One. Work Sheet IV-2 is a working version, for you to complete with your own colors.

Disease	Color	Disease	Color
Acne		Hepatitis	
Alcoholism		Impotence	
Anemia		Jaundice	
Arthritis		Measles	
Asthma		Menstrual Cramps	
Boils		Mononucleosis	
Burns		Nervousness	
Cerebral Palsy		Phlebitis	
Colds and Flu		Polio	
Constipation		Rheumatism	
Diabetes		Varicose Veins	
Fatigue		Venereal Disease	
Headache			

Work Sheet IV-2
Your Correspondences between Diseases and Colors

THE WEB OF THE WYRD

We believe that psychic links interconnect all living things on something like a great psychic Internet. All you have to do to influence someone is to know their right "address"—in this case, a psychic link—and use the appropriate mind keys to tune your transmitter to their frequency or color. Their auric shield will not admit messages that are of the wrong frequency. If their receiver is tuned to a classical station, you don't want to send at the frequency of the local rock station. Generally the aura of a sick person will reflect the illness. If the person is of your culture and generation, that will be the same color that you yourself naturally associate with their illness. If the target is a stranger, try working first with the traditional colors. If the target is of another culture, ask someone of that culture what is appropriate. Occasionally you can get good results if you get a piece of the target's clothing just after it has been worn and before it has been washed or cleaned, and ask your pendulum what color the aura is. The best possible solution is to have someone who sees auras tell you the color of the target's aura.

When you send that healing message out on the psychic Internet, it strengthens the psychic link between you and the target. Capable occultists who can actually see such links say that the link glows with the message and changes color (frequency) with the intent. Your psychic work for the patient's healing intimately connects you with them during the actual time of the work. Psychic energy can flow in both directions along the link. This means, for example, that you may get the target's illness in the case of a healing; or you may get love emotions for another person (the target's desired one). So it is sensible to do the ritual and move away from the frequency that connects you to the target as quickly as possible.

In some cases you can move the target's frequency into a less dangerous area by doing such things as giving them a gift or making sure they have a pleasant time before they go to bed. In many cases, though, as in Alicia's, you have no influence over the target person. Then you should use the traditional table and put out your intent at a level that will break through their auric protective field. This means that in general you should use three times the amounts shown in Table IV-1. This phenomenon is known as the energy spillover effect. Figure IV-1 shows how it works.

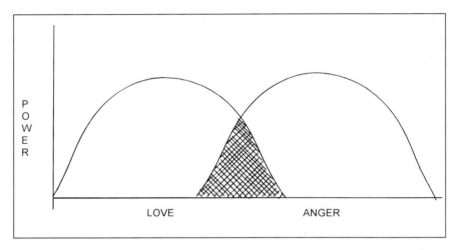

Figure IV-1
Energy Spillover Effect

Modifying Your Intent

Alicia's intent was simple: Save the huskies. She learned that one of her targets had a fiery temperament. A fellow huskie-fancier told her, too, that his aura routinely looked reddish-brown. Now she wanted to modify her intent to get through the reddish-hued aura. All she did was add to her intent a visualization of the dogs' distress and unhealthful situation. The overriding intent was still "Save" but now she knew she was working to save them from something that was in the reddish, anger, blood-disease part of the spectrum. Using that modified intent, she could get through to her target, who it turned out was also in the throes of marital disharmony.

You can compare this to trying to change the mind of someone who simply isn't listening—isn't hearing what you're saying. You must change your argument into something that *does* get through their closed ears into their closed mind. Telling a religious person that Wicca is a better spiritual path (for you) simply doesn't work—but it may be that you can change their path slightly by using Bible quotes about tolerance and "all from the same spirit" or "go a second mile" or "because you have rejected knowledge I reject you."[2] This way you tune yourself to their frequency.

Conclusion

It may seem as if there are an overwhelming number of ways a ritual can fail; yet all the reasons for our suggestions are logical and easy to understand. Once you understand them, there is no reason why your work should disappoint you. Work Sheet IV-3 is a simple checklist for you to complete as you move into your ritual.

Step	Check
Define Intent	
Basic Timing	
Distance	
Number of Workers	
Tuning	

Work Sheet IV-3
Your First Ritual Checklist

You have the power. You are beginning to have the knowledge. Your own confidence in what you can do will see you through.

---

[2]Respectively I Corinthians XII:4; Matthew V:41; Hosea IV:6.

CHAPTER FIVE

ENHANCING THE HIGH

CAUTIONARY TALES

Every Wiccan who practices the art of "bending the future" has a cautionary tale to tell. The practitioner who clapped two candles together and burned himself, and as a result a house burned down . . . the women looking for more males in their coven—who worked a ritual and got an influx of gay men because they failed to stipulate heterosexuals . . . the money ritual where the worker got a sizable check from his employer on the day he was laid off.

Such surprises happen because of an unfocused, ill-defined intent. An unclear intent and insufficient focusing leave enough slack for alternate solutions to occur.

MIND KEYS

Since time immemorial, workers of magic have used various techniques and aids to turn themselves on and to link their intent with their desire. Anything and everything has served to concentrate their attention, to exclude from their awareness everything irrelevant to the work of the moment. Effective focusing changes a general, scatter-gun approach to a rifle-like approach that aims a carefully designed bullet at a single, clearly defined target.

Such *mind keys* tune the mind to the task at hand, ideally eliminating extraneous thoughts. Many of our previous books have given complete *tables of correspondences*. These are the old, old traditional mind keys. Some of the tables are too complex for those of us who just want to do a simple ritual; they can be simplified as Appendix One, Table 4 shows. We always recommend that workers construct their own personal tables. At in-person lectures we find that things which trigger one person to anger (for example) may be just laughable to another. Yes, the sound of a mosquito in the bedroom at night, or the bounced check, or the attitude of the car mechanic may anger and frustrate everyone; but what about the thing that sends someone ballistic? A famous magical worker told us that a little inbred piss-and-tremble lapdog triggered his anger response; yet the same trigger might mean only amused contempt, even pity, to another worker. Modern computers are a great source of generated anger when that latest new wondèrful program that you put on locks the whole thing up.

Let us consider those things that will focus your twenty-first century mind on a particular intent. You have at least five senses. Most people think in pictures—they mentally "see" or *visualize* what they're thinking of. But some people do not see; they may hear, smell, taste, or feel. Many years ago one of our editors reading this suddenly realized that he had a well-developed sense of psychic hearing. He called Yvonne in the middle of the night to tell her he *heard* her aura—in the form of tinkling bells.

You need always to use mind keys that work toward *your* major psychic response mechanism, whether it be sight, hearing, taste, scent, or simply feeling. A quick way to get a feel for your own response mechanism is to think of a baseball game where someone has hit the decisive home run. Do you

see it like a movie?

smell it like sweat?

taste it like hot dogs and mustard?

hear it like the cheers and the crack of the bat?

feel it like the crowd's emotions?

or if your impression combines more than one of these, which came first?

Now what makes you angry? In each column of Work Sheet V-1, enter something that makes you feel anger.

See	Smell	Taste	Hear	Feel

Work Sheet V-1
Your Anger Mind Keys

Which one of these prompts the most angry feelings? Do you *see* the man who ripped you off, *hear* his words, *smell* him, get a bad *taste* in your mouth, or *feel* the angry energy?

A photograph or a press clipping may stimulate you as a very powerful generator of anger; if so, you might be inclined to enter a reminder of the visual stimulus under *See*. Yet, though they are effective, such specific objects may take you away from the purpose of the ritual. For this reason occultists use color as a *See* key. Hence pure color may be the most effective mind key for *See*-people. There are many different shades of scarlet. Go to the paint store and look at the sample chips. Try to decide which of the scarlets engenders anger or keys you to blood. Or maybe another color, a dirty yellow-green or a rust color, makes you angry; you may be triggered by the rust on your favorite garden shears. A subtle and different color is *blank* if a blank computer screen or a blank look triggers anger.

Move on now to think about *smell*. This is more a trained sense than most. To a farmer, the scent of a good manure heap brings pleasant associations. A city dweller may label the same scent simply awful. In today's culture, the scent of tobacco may turn you off because you associate it with lung cancer. What then would replace that scent—in *your* reality—if tobacco is no longer politically correct because of its changed image? Does the *scent* of second-hand baby diapers or vomit make you angry, or does it just disgust you? What odor makes you really furious? Burning oil from an overheated car engine? Cheap hair oil? Bad breath from ill-maintained teeth? Come on. Some smell must really do it to you. What really puts you off the scale? The aftershave your spouse's secret boyfriend wears? The unidentified perfume on your lover's collar?

Do the same for *taste*. You may like chili; perhaps you can imagine the flavor of a batch that should have been delicious but got burned, or some other taste of spoilage. A friend of ours won't eat anything that is "yucky." The actual taste is not important; it's the texture that turns her off. If it's too soft to crunch in her mouth, she spurns it.

What about *hearing*? Some people detest very loud sounds. Because Yvonne has a certain amount of musical training, she loathes people who sing flat, and those who think volume can substitute for clarity. What if someone deliberately over-revs a motorcycle on a quiet street just to annoy people nearby?

Feel—The roughness of burlap? The sharpness of a saw blade? The greasiness of dirty grease with metal chips in it? The prick of a pin? The keyboard that refuses to work? The red-hot radiator cap when the car overheats? The feel of your pants falling down because the new elastic has broken? A dance partner stepping on your toes? Surfaces made sticky by sugar syrup from a spilled soft drink?

Compare your findings with the Mars line in Appendix One, Table 2. Notice how the feeling is linked to colors, gemstones, flowers, and the rest of it.

Ritual ☉bjects

Many years ago a weight doctor recommended a diet that consisted of having a large lump of fat—ten pounds or more—sitting in the front of the fridge. Before eating anything, the dieter took the fat in his bare hands and played with it as he would have molded clay. The intent here was to turn the dieter off from putting repellent stuff like that into his or her own body.

What you need is something to handle in the ritual that will similarly fulfill the mind keys—help the mind get straight to the intent and the target of the ritual without distractions and without traveling along blind alleys.

Main	Secondary	Tertiary	Quaternary

Work Sheet V-2
Your Ritual Mind Keys to Anger

Now that you have a fairly good idea of the sense through which your mind tunes in, complete Work Sheet V-2 with a second set of mind keys that would turn on the anger. This time find four things you could put on your altar with which to do a ritual.

If you *See*, you might enter a photograph in Main, a broken ruby in Secondary, a destroyed water lily in Tertiary, and a statuette of Mars in Quaternary. The visually oriented may substitute photos for any item they cannot obtain firsthand. For a woman doing a sex ritual, a statuette of a god-like youth might suffice. If her need was greater, perhaps a musk-scented pink candle carved in the shape of a phallus would do it. For a male who is visually oriented, pictures of delightful companions could be enough.

If you *Hear*, tape recordings become very useful. A selection from Kurt Weill's *Dreigroeschenoper*, the cries of animals in pain, a car accident? Only you know. Fill in the work sheet in a similar way if you are a *Feeler* or a *Taster* or a *Smeller*.

Beyond the basic mind keys, Table 2 in Appendix One also includes the astrological sign associated with respective intents. In Chapter Seven you will use the signs to work out the appropriate timing for the ritual. Later chapters will expand your list of ritual objects and tools. You can further refine certain of those if you dye the robe an appropriate color, and if you include the herbs in any food you will use during the ritual or if you steep the herbs in the scented oil that anoints your candles.

When you have tentatively decided on certain objects to use in the ritual, sit with them and meditate on them singly. Does each really affect you as you hope, in a way that will intensify the intent?

Mind Keys and Emotion

You may wonder why we chose anger for the two forgoing work sheets. Anger is the traditional scarlet or bright red emotion that is used in treating blood diseases; hence it is an important emotion. For any ritual you will do, you need to figure out not only the best intent, but also the emotion involved, and the associated mind keys that will turn *you* on.

Intent/ Desire	Sight/ Color	Taste/ Flavor	Smell/ Scent	Touch/ Feeling	Emotion Emotion
Wealth					
Love					
Serenity					
General Healing					
Attack					
Luck					
Protection					

Work Sheet V-3
Your Mind Keys for Seven-Plus Intents

It's time to list your own mind keys against the intents in Work Sheet V-3. Notice the two blank spaces in the sheet. In them you will enter any intent not otherwise listed. As an exercise, fill in one of these rows imagining you want to cure high blood pressure using anger. Leave it for a couple of days; then return to it to see whether those keys still set you off.

Understand too that mind keys change with time, and may in fact change almost instantly. The example we often cite is a situation in which you think of blue in connection with serenity and good luck—but then you have a traffic accident with a blue truck, where you get cut and bleed all over yourself. For many months after that, your mind will probably connect blue with danger and even with blood.

Use All Your Senses

Yes, you have one sense that predominates; however, you should learn to use your others. We all have at least five senses, and it behooves us to practice using them all. Even the subordinate ones can serve to reinforce the strongest one. The easiest way to do this is to have someone blindfold and hood you for twenty-four hours. Most of us very quickly find we have an unguessed *proximity* sense, and we learn to trust our subordinate senses when sight is cut off.

Diamond Got Worse

Diamond Y is the third daughter of a traditional Christian family from Tennessee. Her mother had the quirk of naming her daughters after precious stones—Beryl, Ruby, Diamond, Pearl, Garnet, Opal. In her youth Diamond was a rough, tough tomboy and lived up to the image of her name. She was bright, hard as nails, and brilliant at everything she undertook.

She married the lad who everyone assumed was the dullest boy of her high school class. Nay-sayers gave the match only a few months at best. But as sometimes happens, the attraction of opposites succeeded. Winchester and Diamond stayed together and had two pleasant children.

When Winchester was laid off from the strip mine that had employed him, he determined to work for environmental causes instead of for mountain-top removal. Then during a demonstration against the mine "operators"—the plundering landowners—he was shot and killed. Diamond relentlessly pursued the investigation of his death, stirring up endless trouble for herself. Her passion drew the attention of the operators and finally one night a truck ran her and the children off the road. Their car rolled down the mountain-side. The children were relatively unscathed, but Diamond suffered multiple injuries.

Her extended family shared the care of the kids. Despite the good care that the cottage hospital provided, Diamond got worse instead of better. Then a group of mountain Witches worked a heal-ing designed to repair her broken bones and restore her tissues. They too were much surprised in the following days when Diamond continued to get worse, not better.

The Witches asked our advice. We asked what the "regular" doctors had said. Apparently Diamond was suffering only from the broken bones of the accident and had no underlying disease. Still she continued to waste away, not eating and not responding. Eventually we traveled to talk with her friends and—as much as we were allowed—with Diamond herself. During meditation, it became clear that she had simply lost the will to live. Like many hospitals, hers forbade visits from children, and the loss of Winchester and the futility of her efforts against the giant mining corporation had frozen her anger into deep depression.

We prescribed three things: the herb *kava kava*, visits with her children, and a Leo ritual to send her optimistic energy. Almost immediately after the first visit of her children, Diamond began to recover, evincing some interest in having her hair done. Immediately after the ritual she began to want to get out of bed and exercise. Somehow her physicians had missed the fact that depres-sion was causing Diamond's continued negative progress. They had been so concerned with the mechanics of putting her body back together that they had overlooked the thing that nowadays we think of as obvious—her spiritual and emotional needs.

Psychic Links

We have already mentioned that, in common with many occultists, we believe in the Web of the Wyrd—that every living thing is invisibly linked to every other living thing, and perhaps also to some inanimate objects—by something comparable to a psychic Internet. Some cultures believe that when someone gets his photograph made, a tiny piece of that subject stays in the photo, and the Web of the Wyrd extends to the photo. This is why members of many cultures resist being recorded on film. The belief is especially strong in Buddhism and in certain Native American nations. The evil magician who possesses a piece of his target's body can work *sympathy magic* on him.

Anything you touch with emotion retains some of you in it; in fact, these tiny fragments are called *soul pieces.* They always remain connected to you. For millennia workers of magic have used such things as nail clippings and dolls made with the subject's own hair as devices to connect them rapidly to a subject.

Nowadays we call such objects or photographs *psychic links.* A good psychic link can immediately connect you strongly to its "owner" along the Web of the Wyrd. Then you can more effectively send the energy of your intent along a strand of the Web to the target. In every ritual, some form of psychic link will help you activate the Web more easily. It's like having an e-mail address. With a good address you can get there quickly; with an inaccurate one, it may take more time and some frustrating effort.

In the times before photography, when someone wanted the love of a specific lady, they might have a miniature of her painted and carry it near to their heart in a locket. If your ritual is something in the nature of a healing, you can use a direct psychic link to the subject. This may be any possession that the subject has handled and not cleaned, or a photograph. As a last resort, if all else fails, you can very accurately visualize the subject.

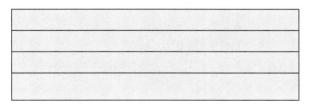

Work Sheet V-4
Your List of Psychic Links

In Work Sheet V-4, list the psychic links you plan to use. Some of them are easy. For a money ritual, enter a piece of gold or a $100 bill. It has to be something that means real money to you. In a ritual for companionship, photographs of yourself and the desired companion can be used, preferably placed face-to-face on your altar.

Understanding and finding psychic links is probably the easiest part of the preparation for your ritual, but you do need to list the links you seek to prevent forgetting them.

CRYSTALS

Certain objects and elements have inherent psychic power. You can call on that power before a ritual, to gear yourself up, and during the ritual as well. Long before crystals and gemstones became fashionable, magicians collected and used them. Shamans have known the powers of gemstones and crystals for hundreds of years. Stones can help to change attitudes, to heal, to increase psychic abilities, and much more. We use them as an adjunct to our work in healing, meditation, scrying,[1] and other activities. Many of us carry them with us to do such things as attract money (tiger eye) and ward off evil (black tourmaline). You can carry more than one type of stone at a time; they *do not* cancel each other out. Carry your stones in a pocket, a bra cup, or a medicine bag pouch fastened to your belt. If you want to *absorb* energy, wear or carry the stone on the same side of your body as your *secondary* hand. If you want to *transmit* the stone's vibration, wear or carry it on the side of your *dominant* hand.

Wearing stones will affect your aura and your links to the Web of the Wyrd, according to the nature of the stones. For example, rose quartz has a very loving vibration. To attract expressions of love to yourself, carry an emerald in your left pocket. To increase the loving vibration in yourself, carry a piece of rose quartz in your right pocket. This is particularly good for people who tend to any sort of heart disease.

---

[1]*Scrying* is the use of some object to quiet your conscious mind while your unconscious furnishes information. A crystal ball, a black mirror, a candle flame, and playing cards are scrying devices.

When purchasing a stone in person, buy the one that you are attracted to, avoiding polished stones if possible. If you are dominantly right-handed, hold it in your left hand.[2] If it feels good to you, it is meant for you and will work for you.

Our Native American friends tell us that each stone has its own spirit; hence you can talk to it and request it to help you in specific ways. Man-made crystals are spiritually dead, so use them only for decoration. Natural crystals are what you want to use in your working. For absolute maximum accuracy in directing the force, use a crystal with a whole, intact point, not a broken point. Broken points give a shotgun blast of energy; energy from a whole point resembles a laser beam in its intensity and focus.

Tricia Moves Back to Arkansas

Tricia W now lives in Hot Springs, Arkansas. She is a powerful psychic healer. She had been living with her husband in New York City. Her fame as a psychic healer rapidly spread, mainly in the Village (Greenwich), and she made a very good living from donations for her work. She found she was getting more and more depleted, and eventually she fell ill. We advised her to cut down on her healing work and increase her energy input by surrounding herself with such things as crystals and herbs, and perhaps sitting inside a pyramid for a few minutes each evening.

When none of these measures seemed really to help her, we suggested she go home to Arkansas for a vacation, to get away from the hustle and bustle of New York.

The vacation worked wonders for her. Unfortunately it also worked wonders for her husband. He found a new love/sex interest, and asked for a divorce. After much emotional negotiation, Tricia

---

[2]Your *dominant* hand is your main transmitter of energy, and your secondary hand is your receiving hand. If you are truly right-handed (not just bullied into being right-handed long ago because it was more convenient for some adult), your right hand is dominant. If you hold a stone in your dominant hand, you will tend to impress your feelings on it instead of receiving its energy. In the hands-across-palm experiment you effectively learned which was your psychically dominant hand.

finally agreed and decided to stay in Hot Springs. Nowadays she is self-employed there, mainly healing horses. It isn't just the mountains that helped her, or the lower population density. She also makes regular visits to the crystal mines, where she spends hours happily digging for crystals. She says, "Sitting in those mountains of dirt with all those imbedded crystals simply recharges me and lifts my spirit."

The Powers in Metals and Woods

Apart from crystals, many natural elements—metals and woods—hold inherent power. Rough pieces of metal ore and rough pieces of wood work better than smooth pieces, especially the metals. Yes, a beautiful locket can enhance the idea of love, both by its shape and because it is composed of a valuable metal. For casting spells, though, you need the metal to be unrefined, in its rough state, and wood chips as an axe might have broken them away from the parent tree. If you are starting with a smooth piece of wood or metal, you can rough up its surface with a file.

Your Guide to the Powers of Crystals, Metals, and Woods

Appendix Table 5 lists typical crystals (or semi-precious stones), woods, and metals you can use for seven intents. Remember, they can

1. charge you yourself; and
2. put energy out to affect others.

Now you can expand your ritual to include sending out natural energy of the appropriate frequency. To do this, at the height of the ritual just drop one or more of them into boiling water or (if they will not be destroyed by heat) drop one into your fire.

Moreover, you can make a piece of jewelry containing the appropriate stone, metal, and wood, to be worn by the target of the spell.

The stone, mineral, and wood interpretations shown in Appendix One, Table 5, are from one of our earlier books. They represent opinions only; they serve to supplement, not to replace, medical advice.

HERBS

Herbs too have their own particular type of energy. Many herbs have quite specific psychic effects distinct from their medicinal properties. Appendix Table 2 shows the traditional psychic effects of herbs. Few of these herbs appear in common herbal remedy books.

The strength of medicinal herbs depends on many factors: At what hour of the day were they harvested? What time of year? Has the season been wet or dry? How much chemical fertilizer has gone into them? Herbs for psychic use must be fresh, with the life force still in them. There are magicians who will not use herbs more than one week old.

In using herbs in ritual, it is quite usual to strew them between the two outermost circles so that their energy will continually bring more power in. You can also include small amounts in the food you eat before and during ritual, and steep them in the oils you use to dress your central candle. Another common way to use herbs is in Native American *medicine bags.* This is the same small bag or pouch you might use to hold stones, crystal, and metal providers of energy. In the Native American context, we take *medicine* to mean *magical power* as *medicine man,* not something to be taken internally to heal an illness.

Especially if you do not know the source of the herbs you propose to use, it is of vital importance to test their psychic output.

FINDING THE POWER OF PSYCHIC TRANSMITTERS

Almost all natural materials emit energy of one sort or another. If you can afford gemstones and other somewhat expensive items, they are the most preferable. Meantime you can gather the odd pebble; some of them are very *hot*—meaning that they put out a lot of energy.

To test the candidate items for their output, "feel" (*psychometrize*) their output with your receiving hand. This can be confusing, and it's relatively easy to fool yourself, because the testing is subjective and not easy. Use this technique:

1. Obtain some small identical opaque containers: matchboxes, pill bottles, or something similar.

2. Into the containers place the items to be tested.

3. Put the containers into an opaque bag and shake them up to mix them thoroughly.

4. Draw them out one at a time and number them.

5. Test each container for five consecutive days, always at the same hour.

6. Fill in Work Sheet V-5.

Object Number	Emotion Felt Day 1	O	Emotion Felt Day 2	O	Emotion Felt Day 3	O	Emotion Felt Day 4	O	Emotion Felt Day 5	O
1										
2										
3										
4										
5										
6										
7										
8										
9										

Work Sheet V-5
Your Ritual Object Energy Detector

In the Day column enter the emotion you feel; at column O enter the level of energy you feel.

Summary

Preparing for a ritual requires that you understand the force you will use. It has its limits; consequently you should not expect it to do more than its nature allows. Fortunately, over the three decades that we have taught its use and had our students experiment with it, we have learned that the simple rules in this chapter generally apply. Tuning yourself and your group to the intent at hand enormously increases your success rate; future chapters will guide you in further refining of your mind keys. If you can persuade a target person (a patient) to wear a medicine bag, make the bag according to information in this chapter. By doing so, you start to influence them, and you also improve their auric state, moving them a little way out of the illness they are experiencing. This should make it easier and less dangerous for you to complete your work.

Anything you might put into your own medicine bag can serve to enhance your ritual as fellow workers add their energy to yours at the height of the procedure.

Chapter Six

Magical Tools and Location

Your Magician's Tools

We cannot overemphasize the importance of making *your own* tools to the *correct measure*. Of course you can buy and own fancy knives and swords; though a few may be suitable for magical work once they are psychically cleansed, your own magical tools made of the correct material and to the right measure with your own labor will work far better.

Consumables and Equipment for Your Ritual

The items you will make or obtain fall into two classes: those for ongoing use, and those for consumption.

1. For ongoing use
   a. the altar
   b. the robe
   c. the athame
   d. the Book of Light (once called a book of shadows)
   e. the chalice and bowls

2. Consumable items
   a. mead
   b. candles and holders
   c. herbs

Many purchased items also serve in a ritual, such as sulfur, sea or kosher salt,[1] copper sulfate,[2] rain or spring water, charcoal, matches, a tape deck, non-magnetic chairs, a bundle of sage made into a *smudge stick*, a recorder[3] or a flute or bell. Any commercial fan will serve; some groups use a bird's wing. If you decide on something like this, remember that it is illegal to have in your possession the parts from certain animals; and any such parts may have negative feelings attached to them.

Take care in the purchase of these needs. If you have trouble, try again another day. You want only good energies or no energies imbedded in them. If there is a problem with the vendor, don't proceed. The tool will remind you, at some level, of the conflict every time you use it.

Our students have done extensive research on the making of equipment for rituals. The methods and materials recommended are the ones they have found to be most comfortable and convenient; however, you may find it easier to use other materials and methods. The making of the tools should be a pleasure, not a problem.

BASIC REQUIREMENTS

No animal material is used. You cannot know how a given animal died. If it died in pain and terror, its feelings will cling to the material. When you approach an object derived from an animal, it is quite possible that you will feel an upsurge of anger or terror. These emotions are often the result of the death throes and terror of an animal. The same reasoning applies to the use of new materials. Who can tell what may have happened to an old knife or chalice?

---

[1] This type of salt has a different crystalline structure than common table salt.
[2] This common garden chemical is a poison, but you will have trouble only if you have a cut on your feet or hands. If you prefer, you can substitute salt dyed blue. If there is moisture in the atmosphere, copper sulfate can stain carpeting. Be careful if you use it indoors.
[3] Vertical flute.

Negative feelings may pervade it. For some reason these emanations do not seem to cling to vegetative materials.

We use non-ferrous materials and no closed metal rings. Time and time again dedicated psychic workers have attested that ferrous metals and closed rings interfere with their work; and Caesar's *Commentaries* report that in earlier times in northern Europe, the peoples in lands he occupied locked up all ferrous metals before a ritual.

The heavy magnetic properties of a sword blade seems to disturb the forces; thus, a bronze or aluminum athame (ceremonial knife) is much to be preferred to a steel one. It is also well known that the forces are so weak that they can become entangled and lost in a knot. With care, the sewing of a garment results in continuous threads whose ends can be held in place by turning them back on themselves without knots, or the garment can be glued along every seam line with fabric glue which outlasts the life of the garment. Synthetic materials and silk build up static electrical charges that also interfere with the work, so again, avoid them.

During the manufacture of the tool, if you get frustrated or injure yourself, give up with this one and start over again. You should put happy pleased parts of yourself into the equipment. Some people make extremely elaborate tools for their first ritual; with others less skilled, the tools appear crude. It is interesting to observe how, over the years, those who have made flamboyant tools make new ones which are toned down, and those with crude tools make new and better ones. The more care (not skill or artistry) that is put into the tool, the more meaning it possesses and the better it will work.

THE SACRED MEASURE

The science of archaeology has a new branch: astroarchaeology. In the past half-century astroarchaeologists have uncovered many new facts about ancient monuments. One of the most fascinating of these facts is that all old monuments were built to a common (shared) standard of measurement. More than 50,000 monuments have been measured. It has been found that all—without exception—use the same standard of measurement, which is now known as the

Megalithic Yard (MY). That Yard is 2.718 feet,[4] approximately 2¾ feet, in length. It is defined forever in the ancient stones.

Since ancient peoples did not have accurate gauges to pass the Measure down to their children, they used other methods to assure that each successive generation would remember the Measure. These mnemotechnics, as they are called, come down to us in such things as the size of the Circle, the standard hands, and the length of the athame blade. To magicians the Measure is sacred. We make our tools and cast our Circles to precise lengths; to break the Measure is to break a link that stretches back to our very roots in the dawn of human prehistory.

Dimensions of all tools and magic circles should be as close as possible to the sacred Measure, and should incorporate the idea behind preserving it. The measures are shown in Table VI-1.

Measure	Decimal Inches	Inches	Metric Cm.
Standard Hand	3.94	3¹⁵⁄₁₆	10.0
Sacred Hand	4.675	4¹¹⁄₁₆	11.87
Megalithic Yard	2.718 ft	2 ft 8⁴¹⁄₆₄ in	82.9

Table VI-1
Measures for Tools and Circles

THE ALTAR

The altar is just a small table so that participants with poor backs, aging bones, or creaky knees can reach the ritual equipment without difficulty. As you know by now, certain woods put out their own energies and materials can absorb energies from a ritual. Make your altar of at least five different woods, one MY high and one MY square; or, if you are an accomplished woodworker, one MY round. Remember, no iron or steel; and the glue should be waterproof so the altar can be washed down after a ritual.

---

[4]The American foot is within 2 percent of the ancient foot at the latitude of Washington, D.C. The ancients used a foot that was earth commensurate; it was derived by dividing the length of a degree of latitude in feet at the site by the length of a year in days. See Chapter Nine.

THE ROBE

Make your robe from white or off-white (unbleached) linen or cotton fabric. Flannel sheet-blankets are an ideal source of fabric. For workers of either gender, a pattern for a man's dressing gown serves well as a cutting guide. The robe should reach to midcalf and must have wide sleeves and a high neck. The overlap at the front should be generously full. A belt of the same material should be long enough to cross at the side and clip to itself. The clip used is usually a piece of copper wire formed into a shape resembling a large paper clip.

It may help to visualize a medieval monk's robe; that is very similar to the robe we use, except that ours opens all down the front.

If you dye your robe in a color appropriate for the ritual, strive to use plant dyes. A glimpse into the world of textiles and dyeing will encourage you to use natural dyes more often; you may even grow your own dye garden.[5] That can be done in a remarkably small space. When you do so you will be following in the tradition of thousands of generations of dyers, making use of the ancient knowledge—which you can extend through your own activities. It's easy, it's fun, and you can also invent new dyes of your own from such things as walnut husks and onions.

THE ATHAME

Begin[6] with a piece of bronze or aluminum ¼ inch thick, 1 inch wide, 9 inches long. On squared paper draw an outline like the one in Figure VI-1. Transfer it with carbon paper to the metal. Grind away the excess metal, or use a hacksaw to remove it. File the blade; then grind it and hone it until it really shines. Get that edge as sharp as possible. The handle end can conveniently be left in rough-finish state. The guard (Figure VI-2) should fit well and tightly, and should be as well polished as the blade. For both blade and guard use successively a coarse file, a fine file, a jeweler's file, emery paper, a leather belt impregnated with fine grinding paste, and a leather belt with jeweler's rouge.

---

[5] R. Buchanan, *A Weaver's Garden* (Dover).
[6] An athame kit is available from Godolphin House, P.O. Box 297-B, Hinton, WV 25951, and on the web at www.wicca.org.

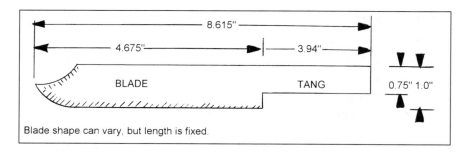

Figure VI-1
The Athame Blade

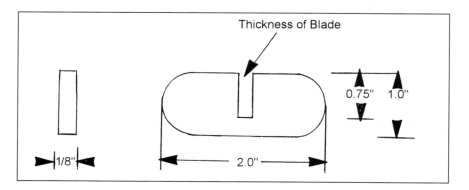

Figure VI-2
The Guard

When the blade is highly polished, it can be etched. Clean it in alcohol and suspend it in a container of melted beeswax by a cord around the tang. Leave it for about ten minutes; then withdraw it and hang it up to cool. You should have a thin, uniform layer of wax all over the blade. With a sharp pointed object, draw the following signs in the wax:

1. The double S for spirit and soul

2. Your secret ritual name number (see section following)

3. The pentagram, whose five points represent the four elements and spirit

4. Your own astrological birth sign

5., 6. On one side the sun; on the reverse the moon

(The number/symbol shown are for an example only. When etching your athame blade, you will use your own name number and your own true birth sign.)

The signs are drawn on each side of the blade with number 1 at the top and 5 or 6 at the bottom. All the signs will appear right side up when the athame is thrust into the ground, as in Figure VI-3.

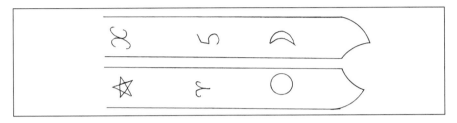

Figure VI-3
Signs Engraved on Blade of Athame

Now suspend the blade in hydrochloric (muriatic) acid or (for brass) nitric acid. Work outdoors when you handle these corrosive acids. Wear heavy industrial rubber gloves. The seal of the wax to the blade and the timing of the etching are critical. If you have some spare scraps remaining from the piece which supplied your blade, make a trial run first to get the feel of the process. The usual etch time for aluminum and new concentrated hydrochloric acid is about seven minutes. After etching, wash the blade to remove the wax and give the blade a final polishing.

From a piece of wood from the dead limb of a tree, or any other scrap wood, make a handle as shown in Figure VI-4.

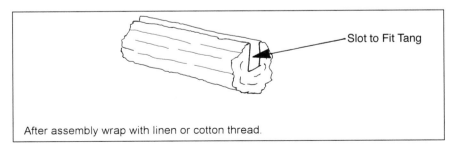

Slot to Fit Tang

After assembly wrap with linen or cotton thread.

Figure VI-4
Handle of Athame

Trial-fit the guard and this piece onto the tang. When the pieces fit snugly, mix up some two-part epoxy glue and glue them together. Then bind the handle tightly with linen thread. Again, finish the binding without knots by tucking the ends under. The athame is now finished; wrap it in clean linen or cotton.

SELECTING YOUR SECRET NAME AND NUMBER

When you do magical work it is usual to use a secret name, so a would-be attacker can gain no link to your magical persona. The name you select should reflect the real you, or the you that you wish to become in the future. Once you have chosen your name, you can calculate its numeric value. Table VI-2 shows the values of individual letters.

1	2	3	4	5	6	7	8
A	B	C	D	E	U	O	F
I	K	G	M	H	V	Z	P
Q	R	L	T	N	W		
J		S			X		
Y							

Table VI-2
Numerological Values of Letters

Let us say you have picked *Sylvius* as your secret name. Figure VI-5 shows how to calculate the secret name number. If you choose to explore the subject of numerology or *gematria* further, it is well covered in our book on prediction.[7]

S   Y   L   V   I   U   S
3+ 1+ 3+ 6+ 1+ 6+ 3   = 23 = 2 + 3 = 5

Figure VI-5
Calculating Your Name Number

---

[7]Frost and Frost, *The Prophet's Bible* (Weiser).

MAKING THE BOOK OF LIGHT

We prefer to call the book of shadows the Book of Light(s). It is a simple binder to keep a record of your rituals and work, and such things as your recipes for bread, good suppliers of herbs, and any other notes, together with (most importantly) the *results* of your rituals. It is pleasant to enter the information in the binder with a broad-nibbed artist's pen in India ink. (Here might be a chance for any calligraphers to show off their stuff.) This both gives an antique look and keeps the verbiage (the verbal diarrhea) down to a minimum. Large bold type or writing makes it easier to read the book in dim light during a full-moon ritual.

If you want to make your own book: the book is usually large, often with pages of parchment-type paper, 12 inches by 16 inches. Craft the covers of thin plywood covered with linen cloth. It is bound by a single strand of hemp rope. As you fill each sheet, fix it with varnish or a spray of plastic fixative leaving it impervious to rain.

Like the other implements, when not in use, the book is kept wrapped in a cloth of cotton or linen.

THE CHALICE AND BOWLS

If you are a potter or a wood turner, you may make these yourself. Otherwise purchase nice articles of glass or wood. If glass, use an etching kit to tune it to your ritual. Whether you make or buy wooden bowls, ritualize them by burning into them appropriate symbol(s).

The most attractive bowls we have ever seen were turned from wood from a tree that has *calluses*. When you cut them off you will get *burl* wood. That gives a very attractive bowl with grains running in many directions.

CONSUMABLES

The items most frequently produced are the consumables. At each ritual we drink mead and eat bread and honey. If you have fasted in anticipation of the ritual, then plan and arrange to have a pleasant, restorative meal afterward. There is nothing special about either product; ideally you will buy or make some dark or whole-grain bread and use honey from a local apiarist.

MAKING MEAD

Mead, in Welsh *methyglin*, is made at least six months in advance of the meeting, and you will want to maintain a constant preparation cycle. It is usual nowadays to make it in five-gallon lots because the requisite spring water comes in five-gallon containers. Preparations call for a container that can boil at least two gallons of water, and an additional five-gallon container. All the containers must be absolutely clean, because any acetic bacteria in the mead will turn it to vinegar.

Besides the containers, you will need these items:

- 5 gallons spring water from local springs
- 16 pounds of honey from local beehives
- pared rinds of 8 lemons
- 6 one-gallon glass bottles
- 1 ounce yeast (a wine yeast is ideal, but common bread yeast will do)
- cotton batting
- a little plastic film wrap
- plastic tubing 1/4 inch by 4 feet

In each five quarts of water, boil four pounds of honey and the pared rinds of two lemons for two minutes. When it is cool to the touch pour it into a glass spring-water bottle. Repeat this operation until all five gallons are boiled and poured back into the spring-water bottles and one of the one-gallon bottles. Break up the yeast and float it on the surface. Place the bottle in a location where it can rest at a constant warm temperature: perhaps a kitchen cupboard. If it is in daylight, cover the bottle with brown paper. Do not cork the bottle tightly because the yeast will soon begin to give off carbon dioxide, and you probably don't need a sticky honey mix coating the walls and ceiling of your cupboard. Use a leak plug of cotton batting covered with plastic film wrap and tied down (Figure VI-6).

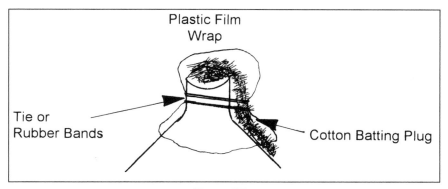

Figure VI-6
Leak Plug

If fermentation has not started after forty-eight hours, add more yeast. After one month, use the plastic tubing to siphon off the upper liquid into the one-gallon containers (Figure VI-7). Be careful to leave behind the sludge in the bottom of the fermentation container. Cover these similarly with plastic film wrap and cotton plug to allow for gas escape. The mead will slowly clear; usually three months in a cold place will do the job. If it is still very cloudy after two months, put each bottle into the refrigerator for a week. When it is clear, siphon it off again into clean one-gallon bottles and cork tightly.

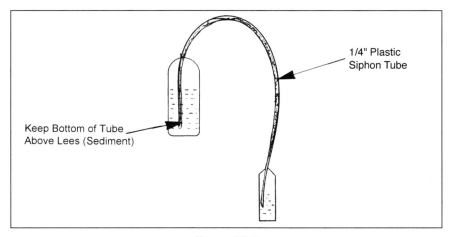

Figure VI-7
Siphoning Mead

CANDLES AND HOLDERS

The easiest candles to make are simply wax poured into old frozen-juice containers, with a wick suspended in each. Bulk wax and wick material are available from any good craft store. You need to add an appropriate color and scent to the wax, and you can also add a small quantity of the appropriate herb.

The most simple candle holders are made from one-quart Mason jars. If you like, you can cut off the threaded section and grind the top smooth. Then you can etch them with symbols appropriate to their proposed location in the circle or other ritual space. Mason jars are certainly sturdy and, given even a modicum of common sense, are fairly heat-resistant.

CLEANING EQUIPMENT OF PSYCHIC NOISE

If a tool has any negative feelings about it or has been in a fairly "heavy" ritual, it needs to be psychically cleansed. Let it rest in a pan of boiling water for five minutes, and then freeze it for thirty minutes. Repeat these steps three times, and all impressed feelings will be removed. In a similar way you can clean your altar and ritual spaces by washing them down with the hottest salted water you (and they) can endure.

You do not need to follow our instructions slavishly for making tools and equipment. You can make do with alternative pieces of equipment. During the Burning Times, when the slightest suggestion of anything that smacked of Witchcraft was a death sentence—probably after horrendous torture—Witches made do with any household object. For instance, they would use a kitchen knife for their athame, drawing the symbols on it in wax and soot. Any bowl or saucer would do for a water container, and any bottle for a flask.

LOCATION, LOCATION, LOCATION

The title here is sometimes called the mantra of the realtor. What is true in real estate is even more important in magical working. The Witch, the sorcerer, the magician know their area and should refrain from conducting rituals in other areas. This is not to say they should not *participate in* the circles of other workers; just that knowing their own area, they can find the points of highest psychic energy in which to work. Keep in mind three basic factors as you decide on a location for your ritual:

1. The geomancy of the place
2. The security and privacy of the place
3. Availability

GEOMANCY

Geomancy is the science of using the energy of the *geod* (planet Earth) in ritual. *Mancy* means to refashion existing events or physical conditions. With equal validity, geomancy could be called *place magic* or *earth magic*. Place magic is deep, coming from the earth itself. The magician's art of using such energy can be compared to using an ordinary light switch. The switch determines whether that enormous power is turned on or off—if you know the simple secret of how to operate the switch. In magical work the switch is *bioplasmic energy*—energy volunteered from human beings. Typically practitioners can dance or spin in the earth field, cutting the lines of force with their own fields to produce large amounts of energy. This we call the *Human Earth Dynamo Effect* (HEDE). Earth magic starts slowly and heavily; but once it starts rolling, it is no more easily stopped than an avalanche. Once it begins moving, it rolls on until the magic is completed.

At certain places in the world it is easier to use this energy than others. At such places you can pick up the energies that are radiated to the earth. Often energy can be found at anomalies in the earth's crust. Geological faults, certain areas near rivers, and peaks of special hills or mountains are power places known to the psychically aware. Many of the world's greatest population centers are located at or near faults. The New York–Washington, D.C. megalopolis and the bustling state of California both run along major fault lines. People instinctively gravitate toward geological fault lines because they feel more energetic when near them.

Carlos Castaneda's chosen place of power in California lies atop a known geological fault.

PLACES OF POWER

1. Intersections (man-made faults), where ideally four or more roads meet

2. Hills, on the center hilltop of three or more hills. Tall buildings work as artificial hills.

3. Fault line
   a. At east/north end
   b. Across fault
   c. On the higher rim

4. River and springs

MAP DOWSING

If local maps do not show underground streams and fault lines, the power points in a given area may not be readily apparent. Get a map of the area, as large-scale as you can find. Turn it over. Lay a straightedge along the bottom edge, and very slowly slide the straightedge upward across the map's "wrong" side. Have a helper observe a pendulum and tell you when it indicates something. At the pendulum's reaction, lightly draw a pencil line across the map at that point. Cover the whole map, bottom to top.

Now do the same from the right-hand side. Lay the straightedge down parallel to the edge of the map, and move it slowly leftward. Again, let the second worker notify you of any deviation in the pendulum's motion. Go right across the map with light pencil lines.

Where lines intersect, push a pin through the map. When you turn the map over, you will have several locations of psychic high points to investigate.

LEY LINES

The ancients mapped the known world and drew lines along many earthly power lines. Along those lines they placed markers of foreign stone, five markers per mile; and at every 2.72 miles they placed a major ceremonial site. Places where these *ley lines* intersect are points of phenomenal power. Many such ley lines and power points have been rediscovered and remapped by the British *Ley Hunters Society* and its founder Alfred Watkins.

The very ancient site of Glastonbury, sacred to Celtic Witches, a site of annual pilgrimages, is the place where no fewer than eight ley lines intersect. One line starts at Canterbury, runs precisely through Stonehenge, and ends at Glastonbury. This system of power lines is not new; it has been known to "in" people for hundreds of years.

MANUFACTURING YOUR OWN POWER POINTS

Ley lines, geological faults, rivers, mountain tops are all sources of energy. To gain bounteous energies you may travel to these arcane sites to gather geomantic energy; it is available for the asking. Perhaps, though, you live in a house or an apartment. How can you find or create a point within your reality that will let you tap into the geomantic energy?

Any discontinuity will do it. Witches have traditionally worked at the intersections of roads. Any road constitutes a man-made geological fault. Walls of houses and apartments are similarly artificial fault lines. Thus the way to construct an artificial ley line is to start at a doorway in your dwelling. Place large foreign stones that you have gathered from a river, at intervals of 2.72 feet, in the form of a cross. Make the center of the cross in the doorway. Do your ritual at the intersection.

Your apartment house constitutes an artificial hill. If you have access to its roof, you can do your ritual there. With a little ingenuity, you can create a simulated river in your apartment and use its flow to aid you in charging.

FAR FROM THE MADDING CROWD

There are many ritual sites which don't seem to occur to the average occultist. We recommend national and state parks. Most of them have small cabin spaces with fire pits and isolated areas where you can work. This is not a necessity, but in spring and summer and in early fall it's very pleasant to be outdoors and away in a psychically clean area to do your work. If you have a relatively unused space, either in or out of doors, in or near your home, that space can be made adequate for the work. Such a space should

1. have a minimum of clutter,

2. have walls that can be washed down,

3. have a smooth floor,

4. be at least 15 feet square,

5. be close to a power point (either natural or artificial), and

6. be constructed with an absolute minimum of ferrous metal.[8]

7. Have areas nearby that can be set up as private bowers for intimacy.

It is best that the walls of any room where you do such work be plainly painted with a washable latex paint. After any ritual they should be washed down with a solution of one gallon of heated spring- or rainwater to which you have added a cup of salt. Remember that not only the walls and the floor must be washed, but also the ceiling. In cases where very heavy rituals have been done, after the washing the room may have to be *smudged*. Burn at least two pounds of sage in a charcoal brazier and let the smoke saturate the area. Again, as in dyeing (above), you may eventually want to grow your own sage.

If even this cleansing of the ritual space does not entirely remove the imbedded emotions, the only cure is time. For several months any ritual working should be moved elsewhere. This is why Witches tend to move from site to site instead of having a permanent ritual setup. There has been a general move in the community—partly generated by laziness and partly by lack of awareness—for people to have ritual "rooms" where they do all their work. We feel this is a mistake.

---

[8]We have often been amused by the surprise that westerners express when they learn that a Japanese company building steakhouses insists on construction without nails. Now you too know the reason.

CHO HOI MOVES FROM HIS HOUSE

Cho Hoi is a middle-aged Chinese gentleman living now in Burbank, California. He was always concerned about the chronic drained feeling he got whenever he entered his former dwelling. He had lived in Malibu in a house that overlooked the Pacific Ocean, a most fashionable and desirable location, and one that many people in the entertainment industry wanted. He never could figure out why the house worried him. There had been no previous occupants, and he wondered whether an underlying fault meant that the house would slide into the ocean. But surveys showed there was no such problem.

He had his elderly parents over from Taiwan. His father took an instant dislike to the house. He told Cho Hoi that the house was badly arranged on feng shui principles, and that from a geomantic point of view its location was a disaster. It was on the downside of a tee intersection where a long straight road from the hills ran almost to the front door. Energy would flow from the hills behind and right through the open-plan house, taking energy from occupants as it went. He suggested immediately closing off the front door and placing a large mirror behind it. More to mollify the old man than anything else, Cho Hoi tried it—and of course the house immediately felt better. He asked the senior man then what else he could do. The father's answer was succinct: "Move."

Cho Hoi had many friends in the film industry. Of them, many had admired his house. When he mentioned at the studio that he was thinking of selling, several people expressed interest. One, a particular old friend, lived in Burbank in a smaller house. Cho Hoi's father checked it out and said it lay on the edge of a fault line. Cho Hoi decided to exchange residences; along with all the other benefits, this meant a significant financial adjustment in his favor.

Cho Hoi now has a happy home.

EDDIE, CHARLAYNE, AND BRUSHWOOD

Brushwood Folklore Center near Sherman, New York, enjoys a beautiful setting where people gather to explore "alternative" interests they share and to camp out. Many pagans, Witches, and alternative spirits visit there. They are secure enough to be clothing-optional. The campsite is in a gentle valley where a small sluggish stream flows. Many inexperienced workers do their rituals in the valley on the right-hand bank of an east–west stream; they fail to realize that the moving water does not overcome the disadvantage of working in the bottom of the valley. More advanced workers, like Eddie and Charlayne though, climb up out of the valley onto the top of a local hillside to do their work, and many camp there forgoing the convenience of running water and well-trodden paths, all for the sake of the advantageous geomantic location.

LEGAL OCCUPANCY

Most federal and state parks have a permitting system. Through it you rent a space for a fixed amount of money for a fixed time. It is important that you clearly state to the permitting agency that you intend to do a ritual, hold a church service, or do other *religious* activities. (*No surprises* is an excellent policy here, as on many other occasions. It may amount to "Get there first with your side of the story.") Someone may get a clue from your organization's title that this is Wiccan/pagan or alternative, or they may not. Your statement that this is a *church* activity should protect you when some fundamentalist bean counter suddenly discovers that you are (gasp) Witches and his god tells him he is to cancel the permit—or do something more drastic. People who feel fear can get inventive and dangerous.[9] Such occurrences pop up all the time, whether out of fear or of ignorance.

A Ramada Inn in Springfield, Missouri, (illegally) canceled out a Wiccan church meeting at the last minute on the excuse that they "needed the room" because they had had a "sudden increase in sign-ups for a convention." Church lawyers advised us that the flimsy, transparent excuse probably would not have stood up in court; but because of the cost of suing, we did not pursue the matter. At least they canceled with enough time remaining that we could find another ritual space. Their actions were, however, definitely illegal

---

[9] We are not alone in having had an actual bomb in a hotel where we gathered and bomb threats at several others.

and discriminatory. Since that time the Church has received a letter of apology from the Inn's management—though that hardly compensates for the disturbance their cancellation caused.

Any time you find a ritual space, then, make sure that you can cover your tail with the necessary paperwork. Be legal (see Appendix Two). Have the paperwork that proves you are legal.

YOUR LOCATION: FINDING A SITE

Work Sheet VI-1 lists various factors to help you grade locations that may meet your requirements. Just as at Brushwood, for many people the convenience of working beside running water outweighs a hilltop location. So for you, especially when considering various options; you may find that the convenience of working in your backyard overcomes the extra psychic boost you would get from a beautiful high hilltop. We are indeed fortunate in West Virginia; when the back-to-nature generation came in, they bought land and many of them set up sacred spaces which fulfill one or more requirements of ideal locations. One such location on a hilltop has large stones (megaliths) set out to enhance its natural hilltop power. Working there one midwinter, when the stars seemed within arm's reach in the bitingly cold weather, made it an unforgettable experience.

Consideration	Location 1	Location 2	Location 3	Location 4
Security				
Space				
Psychic Power				
Legal Occupancy				
Cost				
Other				

Work Sheet VI-1
Assessing Possible Locations

Grade each candidate location for each consideration; just rank on a scale from one to ten. You will quickly identify the best one.

Conclusion

Working a ritual can be a very worthwhile undertaking, especially when it results in a dramatic healing. Making magical tools and spending time searching out a good location may look like a lot of work.

How about giving up one TV program a day, though, until it's done? If you wanted to bake a cake from scratch, starting without one tool or a kitchen, not even a stove or fuel, that too would look like a forbidding task. You are working on something that will mean a lot more to your life than just a cake.

Ancient Chinese proverb say:

Longest journey start with single step.

†iminG

The *timing* of your ritual is critical for many reasons—and the timing may be the most difficult decision you will make; if not difficult, it is at least complicated. But it's all been done by people no smarter than you are, so take it slowly one step at a time.

Consider these factors:

1. When will the sun and the moon be in their best aspects?
2. When will the alignment of the Earth with the wheel of the heavens be most beneficial?
3. When will the patient/target be most receptive?
4. When will the other participants be available?
5. When will the other participants be "high"?

Full Moon, Dark Sun

We tend to think of the moon as being the thing that most affects humans and the tides with its gravitational pull. In fact the gravitational pull from the sun is stronger than that from the moon. It is the *combination* of the sun's forces with those of the moon that causes variations in behavior of the tides and in human emotions. Figure VII-1 shows the full moon on one side of the Earth and the sun on the other, effectively opposite each other. You can see now why it is sensible to plant root crops when the moon is full: The opposing gravitational pulls tend to neutralize each other, and the pull of the sun allows roots to reach downward more easily. Similarly in Figure VII-2 you see that at noon on a day of new moon the sun and the moon are aligned, maximizing their pull and encouraging plants to grow upward. That is why you plant flowering crops at that time.

In many ways the moon serves as an indicator of the sun's position. The aligned sun and *new* moon pull upward; the sun and the *full* moon pull in opposite directions; and at the two quarters *(quadratures)*, sun and moon pull at right angles to each other (Figure VII-3).

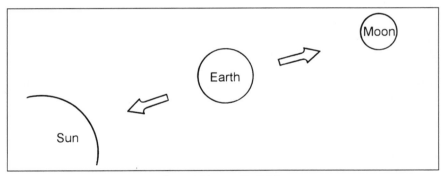

Figure VII-I   Full Moon

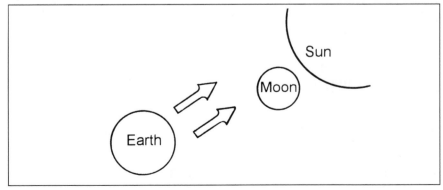

Figure VII-2   New Moon

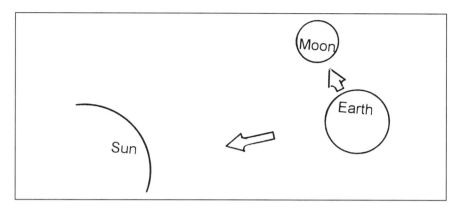

Figure VII-3
Quarter Moons

Moon Phases

As the Earth rotates under the sun and the moon, the effect of their pull on the Earth is far more immediate and apparent than other energies arriving from the further reaches of the cosmos. The pull causes the tides of the ocean to rise and fall. With such an inexorable effect on fluids, it is easy to see why solar and lunar movements affect the characteristics and the behavior of humans—who dwell in bodies that are 95 percent liquid. If you have a teenager who is due to get a driver's license, sit with the kid outside a hospital's emergency room on a summer full-moon night. Watch what humans do to themselves with their vehicles when the moon turns them into—yes—*lunatics.* This night and its sister night of new moon are the nights when accidents and general craziness reach their terrifying peak.

Witches have known for millennia that you should plant root crops (beets, carrots, all downward-growing vegetables) by the light of the full moon; that upward-growing crops produce better when planted at new moon. Taking this approach a step further, we know that when we want to reduce an effect (such as a swelling) we should work as soon after full moon as possible so that as the moon wanes (grows smaller) the swelling will shrink. We know that if we want to increase an effect such as wealth, we should work as soon after new moon as possible. As the moon waxes (grows),[1] so the effect will magnify.

The moon's maximum effect occurs as it crosses the *zenith*— the midpoint of the sky above your head. That is, it is directly overhead either at approximately midnight (full moon) or at midday (new moon). The effect is not a sudden peak but gradually builds up and changes, so that you can time your ritual for almost any time the moon is above the horizon. In fact, Tantrists schedule all their rituals for three days *after* the appropriate moon phase because they observe that the tides of the ocean are highest three days after the moon's phase. You can see the same effect if you sit in a full bathtub and slide between the tub's front end and its back end. That "slosh" time between your motion and the peak wave at the end of the tub illustrates the three-day *hysteresis* between the moon's phase and the tidal response. Tantrists see a powerful correlation between the tidal rise and human emotional swings.

Figure VII-4 shows the buildup and the dropoff of solar and lunar influence throughout a complete moon cycle. Notice that you have a few days in each half of the cycle in which to work. Timing is important; but, as Figure VII-5 shows, even here you have a window of several hours when the effect reaches maximum. As a general rule of thumb, work within three days and within two hours of the moon's crossing overhead.

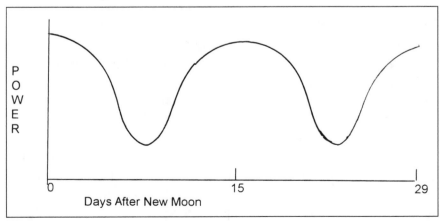

Figure VII-4   Monthly Variations in Moon Power

---

[1]German *wachsen*—to grow.

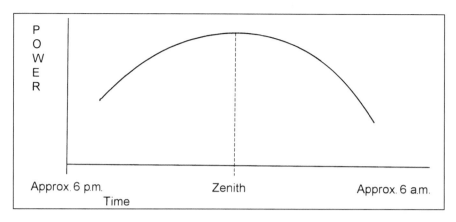

Figure VII-5   Typical Daily Moon Variations

Wynne Died of a Tonsillectomy

Gavin's own great-aunt Wynne died early in the 1930s—of a tonsillectomy. She bled to death. The family's enduring grief troubled Gavin sufficiently that he determined to find out what phase the moon was in when she had her operation. Sure enough, it was the day after full moon. Hospital studies show clearly that something like 80 percent of fatal cases of post-operative bleeding occur within three days of full moon. Thus it is only sensible to avoid any surgery both at full moon and at new.

Keeping in mind the phases of the moon, you can proceed to look at the best time for your ritual. Remember always that if you want something to decrease, you should work at full moon; and if you want something to increase, work at new moon. Some work can be fine-tuned for either direction; for instance, you could do a ritual for *increase in wealth* at new moon—or a ritual for a *decrease in expenses* at full moon.

Deana and Her Refrigerator

Deana is a pleasant lady whom we knew before we moved to West Virginia. At that stage of her life she was working to support two toddlers while her husband was on military assignment overseas. Even with allotments and some coverage of medical expenses, things were not easy. When her ancient refrigerator quit, she bought a new one on a major chain store's credit card. Then she truly had great difficulty in meeting all the payments she had incurred.

At full moon she did a little ritual involving a candle and a metal pyramid; its intent was to diminish her expenditures. Somehow the cost of the refrigerator simply disappeared from the monthly statements relating to her charge card. Coincidence? Magic? Who knows? But those are the coincidences we like. She wore a little smile when she told us the story, but she was dead serious. "I'll *never* take that pyramid off the fridge top!"

Astrological Misinformation

In ancient times astronomers used the sky to gauge the passing of the seasons. They gave the various parts of the sky names that we still use today; often these were taken from fanciful interpretations of star patterns in a specific area of the sky. Thus when the part of the sky that they recognized as Aries was on the eastern horizon at dawn, putting dawn in Aries, they said "We are in Aries. That means it is springtime."

The step into astrology was a very short one, when people noticed that those individuals born at various times of the year exhibited different characteristics. These characteristics were then equated to certain diseases and intents. The *choleric* man was ideal for military work, and he had an overabundance of blood; so his sign ruled military endeavors and the curing of such things as high blood pressure. The first line of Appendix One, Table 2, shows these characteristics. All you need to do is look up in the table the appropriate sign that closely matches your intent.

Over the years various attempts have been made to adjust the calendar and to give each "house" of the zodiac equal duration. (The "house" is the length of time that the sun rises in a specific sector of the sky.) Table VII-1 shows the dates generally accepted in our era, to be assigned to each house.

SIGN	DATES	SIGN	DATES
Aries	Mar 21–Apr 19	Libra	Sep 23–Oct 22
Taurus	Apr 20–May 20	Scorpio	Oct 23–Nov 21
Gemini	May 21–Jun 20	Sagittarius	Nov 22–Dec 21
Cancer	Jun 21–Jul 22	Capricorn	Dec 22–Jan 19
Leo	Jul 23–Aug 22	Aquarius	Jan 20–Feb 18
Virgo	Aug 23–Sep 22	Pisces	Feb 19–Mar 20

Table VII-1
Modern Dates Assigned to Each House*
*Dates vary slightly from year to year.

The constellations of ancient time served as the hands of a giant clock. We still use the same names the ancients gave to those "houses," even though the constellations they knew have shifted in the *precession of the equinoxes.* Today if you look at the dawn horizon on July 25, you will see Castor and Pollux, the twins of Gemini, not Regulus, the principal star of Leo. Nevertheless the astrological differences between people born in the various houses persist, showing that the energy comes from beyond the stars. It may be that *cosmic background energy*, and not the constellations themselves, gives attributes to those born "under their influence."

Energy from Beyond the Stars

Figure VII-6 shows quite clearly how energies from outer space reach the Earth. The circular band of astrological symbols represents the ancient clock that tells you where you are at dawn. Because the Earth rotates on its own axis, on any single day you are briefly exposed to *each* energy source in turn. If you want to do an Arian ritual, perhaps to cure a blood disease, but the sun currently rises in Sagittarius, simply wait several hours past dawn. The Earth will rotate under the wheel of the heavens, and then your location will receive Arian energy.

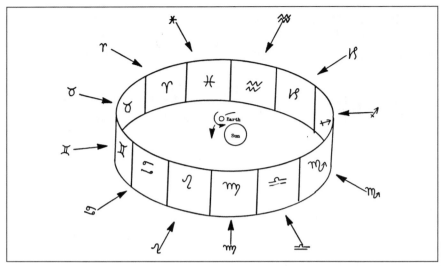

Figure VII-6   Energy from Beyond the Stars

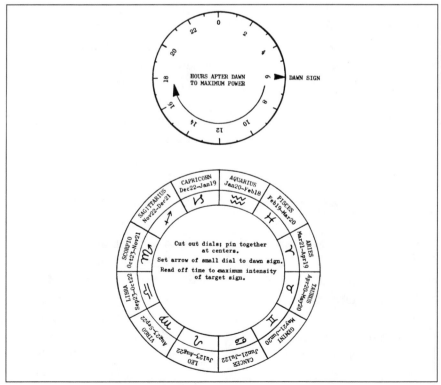

Figure VII-7   Your Energy Power Dial

To calculate the time on a specific day when you will have the correct energy for your ritual, make the Energy Power Dial shown in Figure VII-7.

1. Cut out the smaller dial. Pin it to the center of the larger dial in such a way that the inner dial can rotate inside the outer dial.
2. To find the time interval from the dawn sign to the center of the energy of your target sign: Place the arrow or zero of the inner dial against the date of the full or new moon you plan to use.

3. On that same dial, read the time opposite the center of the sign you plan to use.

Filling In Your Work Sheet

Work Sheet VII-1 lists some fairly obvious items to fill in. The date of ritual depends primarily on the phase of the moon and on the availability of other participants. If you insist on working on a specific night so that a prospective participant must give up their dance class or other activity, that person will not be fully committed to the ritual. Instead (s)he may be thinking of that other activity, and may well resent your insistence. So pick a date that everyone agrees on.

Now complete a work sheet such as the one shown in Work Sheet VII-1.

On Line 1, enter the *intent* of the ritual and check the box for *increase* or *decrease*.

On Line 2, enter *full* or *new*, and *waxing* or *waning*.

On Line 3, consult your almanac to learn the correct *moon date*, and enter the range of best *moon times*; for example, 10 p.m.–2 a.m. or 10 a.m.–2 p.m.

On Line 4, enter the next correct moon date.

On Line 5, enter the appropriate astrological sign.

On Line 6, insert *dawn time* from Table VII-2 (or the local weather channel).

On Line 7, enter *time to correct sign* from your Energy Power Dial.

On Line 8, add Line 6 to Line 7 to learn the optimal time for your work.

DATE	TIME—A.M.	DATE	TIME—A.M.
1 Jan	7:15	1 Jul	4:10
15 Jan	7:10	15 Jul	4:20
1 Feb	7:00	1 Aug	4:35
15 Feb	6:40	15 Aug	4:50
1 Mar	6:20	1 Sep	5:05
15 Mar	6:00	15 Sep	5:25
1 Apr	5:30	1 Oct	5:35
15 Apr	5:00	15 Oct	5:55
1 May	4:40	1 Nov	6:15
15 May	4:20	15 Nov	6:35
1 Jun	4:10	1 Dec	6:55
15 Jun	4:05	15 Dec	7:10

Table VII-2
*Table of Dawn Times**

*When the government plays games with the clocks in summer months and converts Standard Time to Daylight Saving Time, you will need to add one hour to the times above. Example: on 1 June, 4:10 becomes 5:10.

These times are approximate and will vary slightly from place to place. If, for instance, you are on the western edge of a specific time zone, dawn will occur about thirty minutes later than that shown in the table, because the table gives the center of each time zone. Watch your weather channel to learn the actual dawn time *where you live.* If you live in the center of a time zone, the times will be accurate. However, if you live on the edge of a time zone or much further from, or closer to, the Equator, than the central United States, or in the southern hemisphere, there will be a considerable variation in dawn time.

1. Intent ____________________ Increase ❑ Decrease ❑
2. Moon Phase Full ❑ New ❑ Waxing ❑ Waning ❑
3. Best Moon Time 10 p.m.→2 a.m. ❑ 10 a.m.→2 p.m. ❑
4. Next Correct Moon Date __________
5. Appropriate Sign __________
6. Time of Dawn on Moon Date __________
7. Hours to Correct Sign __________
8. Best Time for Ritual __________

Work Sheet VII-1
Work Sheet to Identify Time of Ritual

Let us say that you want to do an Arian ritual on the full moon of January 15. Sample Work Sheet VII-1a is filled in for this ritual.

Look first at Table VII-2. Notice that on January 15 dawn occurs at 7:10 a.m. Place the zero of the inner dial of your Energy Power Dial at the point in Capricorn where you figure January 15 should be; that is, toward the end of Capricorn. Now fill out Work Sheet VII-1. You will see that five and one-half hours later, you will be in the middle of Aries. Totaling these two on your work sheet gets you to 12:40 p.m. as the time for the ritual. Such a time would work for a new moon, not a full, so you must try again.

Timing of Ritual Work Sheet 1

1. Intent Reduce Blood Pressure Increase ❑ Decrease ☒
2. Moon Phase Full ☒ New ❑ Waxing ❑ Waning ☒
3. Best Moon Time 10 p.m.→2 a.m. ☒ 10 a.m.→2p.m. ❑
4. Next Correct Moon Date Jan 15
5. Appropriate Sign Aries
6. Time of Dawn on Moon Date 7:10 a.m.
7. Hours to Correct Sign 5:30
8. Best Time for Ritual 12:40 p.m.

Sample Work Sheet VII-1a
Example

The results of this calculation show that the moon and the astrological aspects do not match. The work sheet has to be reworked, changing from *lowering blood pressure* to *opening arteries*. Sample Work Sheet VII-1b gives an acceptable result.

Changing the intent of the ritual to an *increase* (in this case of blood flow), you arrive at a new-moon date of January 1. Completing the same steps in filling out a fresh work sheet, you get Work Sheet VII-1b and a time of 1:45 p.m. This time is just inside an acceptable limit.

Perhaps neither of these methods will work in your case. If this happens, choose another sign to work in. In the table of correspondences, blood disease is under Venus; so you know that you can usefully redo the work sheets for a Venusian ritual.

Timing of Ritual Work Sheet 2

1. Intent <u>Open Arteries—Increase Blood Flow</u> Increase ☒   Decrease ❑
2. Moon Phase   Full ❑   New ☒   Waxing ☒   Waning ❑
3. Best Moon Time   10 p.m. ➞ 2 a.m.   ❑ 10 a.m. ➞ 2p.m. ☒
4. Next Correct Moon Date   Jan 1
5. Appropriate Sign   Aries
6. Time of Dawn on Moon Date   7:15 a.m.
7. Hours to Correct Sign   6:30
8. Best Time for Ritual   1:45 p.m. (13.45)

Sample Work Sheet VII-1b
Example

A Note to Amateur Astrologers

If you have investigated astrology, you may find it confusing that we have used an equal-house system whereas some astrological systems use unequal houses. Conversely you will find us unusual in our use of real dawn times, whereas the most popular "easy" system uses 6 a.m. as dawn—throughout the year! Using the correct dawn time and equal houses guarantees that you are in the correct energy band with your calculations. It is true that you may not be at the maximum, especially if the ritual is to be done either at midwinter or at midsummer; however, there will be plenty of energy, and correct dawn times and equal houses simplify the calculation. To do it correctly, get your friendly competent astrologer to do a Koch calculation for you.

Getting High at the Right Time

In Chapter Five we mentioned the way your power output varies during any twenty-four-hour cycle. You have now selected a specific day and time for the ritual you want to do. Look back at the work sheet you prepared for Chapter Five. You will see that you may not be at your peak output at the time that is best for the ritual. To change the point at which your personal output is highest, you need to change your *circadian clock*. If you have traveled between time zones, you may already have experienced a derangement of your clock—*jet lag*.

Depending on the time of day or night when your output is at maximum, you can start getting up either a little earlier each day or a little later, until your whole day is adjusted. Getting up earlier or later means that you must also take your meals correspondingly earlier or later. Imagine you have traveled across the continent and are in a different time zone. To figure out how many hours to adjust your schedule, look at Work Sheet VII-2.

---

1. From Work Sheet IV-1, decide on the time that your power output is at a peak.
2. From Work Sheet VII-1, establish the required time of the planned ritual.

Power output peak time   _____
Time of ritual   _____
Time difference   _____
Decide whether your circadian clock needs to go backward or forward. (Use the minimum time difference.)
Number of days to ritual   _____
Divide time difference by number of days _____
This answer is the number of hours or minutes by which you need to adjust your clock per day.   _____

Work Sheet VII-2 — Adjusting Your Circadian Clock

Keep changing your clock until your maximum-power output coincides with the time designated for the proposed ritual. Yes, this will cause some disruption in your life; but again we come back to the idea: How important to you is the ritual and its result? Is it worth the trade-off?

As you learned in Chapter Five besides adjusting your circadian clock, you should fast and be celibate for two to three days before the ritual date.

It is necessary to run similar tests on all the participants to establish the time when they can produce the greatest amount of psychic energy, and get them to adjust their individual circadian clocks so that their peak time will match the time of the ritual. Useful work has been done on this subject; scientists have come to describe people as either *larks*—day people—or *owls*—night people—depending on whether the subjects are bright and energetic early in the day, or whether they get going only after 10 a.m. or noon. Day people are widest awake in the morning, and at that time they have their maximum psychic output. Night people tend to have maximum output in the evening. Getting the two types of people to work successfully in the same ritual takes a certain amount of choreography. All participants in the ritual must shift their circadian clocks and become celibate. If anyone is unwilling to change their body clock, you should probably gently disinvite them.

Rituals for Special Dates

To this point we have discussed rituals designed to change future events. The general name for such activity is *magic*. Another type of ritual has a more otherworldly tone: These are the seasonal festivals, often deeply spiritual, that honor the corners of the year. Some of them, namely the equinoxes and the solstices, fall on solar events; the others commemorate milestones in the agricultural year and follow the moon. Samhain will always occur on the full moon nearest November 1, whether that falls in October or November. This means that Samhain will generally occur in Scorpio—though occasionally it will occur in Libra. Since these rituals are usually observed in the evening or at night, rituals appropriate to Taurus would be in order, because on the zodiacal belt Taurus is opposite Scorpio as evening is opposite dawn.

Great numbers of people attend these seasonal festivals. Because you cannot realistically expect them all to adjust their body clocks to maximum output, you will effectively rely on a large number of weak batteries instead of a few batteries fully charged; but since seasonal rituals usually do not work to change the future in magical ways, that is perfectly all right.

When Their Guard Is Down

In doing a psychic healing, another consideration comes into play. We believe that the body makes itself sick and heals itself, and modern medicine is beginning to agree that at least part of the healing process occurs in the mind. In oversimplified terms, when the hypnotist tells his subject that he has burned them, and touches them with the eraser end of a pencil, a blister appears. Then when he tells the subject that he didn't burn them, instead he touched them with an eraser, the blister disappears. In its simplest form, this is the mind causing a disease and curing it.

You probably will not have the target of the healing in circle with you; so you must schedule the timing for an hour when the subject is open to telepathic suggestion. The easiest time for this is when they are asleep; thus many healings are done at night.

Conclusion

Your completed charts will tell you the best time for a ritual. The first time you use the charts, it may seem a little difficult; but the more often you work with them, the easier it will become. Remember that you need to do this work both for a simple personal ritual and for a ritual involving a large number of participants.

Your work to decide the ideal timing for a ritual will bring a new awareness to you. The great wheel of the heavens revolving overhead will give you a new sense of your own place in the rightful scheme of things. You may find that the adrenaline level of your life will imperceptibly lower as you realize that a lot of day-to-day stuff really doesn't matter all that much in the timeless dance of the stars. We cannot believe this is a bad thing.

CHAPTER EIGHT

THE BIG FOUR

UNIVERSAL QUESTS

We receive thousands of letters and e-mails each year requesting help. Well over 90 percent fall within four categories:

1. Companionship—either "Improve my present relationship" or "Get me a new companion." We turn down all these requests, because any companion we chose would probably not suit the requestor. There is also an *ethical* consideration: Would we be doing a ritual that cages the target?

2. Wealth—"I need a new car, a new job, a new . . ." Well, fill in the blank yourself. Some of these are real needs that have occurred through no fault of the petitioner; these we try to help by giving them *instructions* on improving *their own* situations. Unfortunately, predictably, many such requests are purely whines from people who think *work* is just another four-letter word. Such people we don't help.

3. Health—In most of these cases, if the patient is a member of the Church of Wicca who has worked with a legitimate healing professional, we do our best to help. We never lose sight of two facts:

   a. We must thoroughly investigate the background before we can legally proceed.

   b. Legal considerations mean that we can work only for documented members of the Church of Wicca.

4. Protection—"I've been hexed. My life is in the toilet and it's not my fault." Whether or not the person has really been hexed, it's real to them; unless something is done, they'll continue having a miserable life. The old shaman waves the feathers and rattles the gourds, and his patient is cured of the hex. In modern life, though, the patient wants more: a physical presence of protection, an amulet, a mirror, or anything "real" that they can touch. For a Christian this might be a cross. For someone of an alternative spirituality, it must be something meaningful in *their* reality.

Companionship

THE ETHICS OF COMPANIONSHIP RITUALS

Companionship rituals are inherently *caging* rituals. You are forcing someone to be attracted to you. The general consensus currently is that when you have a great need for a companion, it is all right to do a ritual of a generalized nature, but it is *never* all right to do a ritual that would cage a specific individual. Basically, what this means is that you will put out a general search, if you like, and activate many strands of the Web simultaneously. Some of the strands will result in meetings and attraction, but none of them will be specific enough to cage a particular person.

DEFINING THE INTENT

So you want a companion in your life? Work Sheet VIII-1 will help you define at least a rough draft of the focused picture of the person you hope to bring into your life.

You want love? Is it sexual or platonic? Motherly? Companionable? What about gender? Orientation? Clearly, the answer to the love question, along with your sexual orientation, will combine to define the gender of the person whom you will visualize in your ritual.

Consider carefully, too, your current state of mind. Are you simply hard up and want to get laid? Or do you seek a trustworthy long-term friend with whom you can talk things over? Maybe that would be someone like your friend of school days, your bitching-buddy, from whom you had no secrets, with whom you could talk about anything.

Where does the beauty/physical attractiveness factor come into your ranking of desirable features? Does it outweigh personality? What about intelligence? Is your ideal as sharp as you are, or maybe dumber? How about integrity? How about abilities and skills? Are you the right-brain artistic type needing someone to organize you? Or are you an organizer who longs for someone to widen your artistic horizons? Where do you fall on the spendthrift/miser scale? Can you live without music? Or stock-car races? Or birdwatching? Or your electronic toys?

So now you have defined this intelligent, blue-eyed punk/bombshell/heartthrob/knuckle-dragger/buddy/whatever you like. How much further do you want to go in your definition? Does it need more fine-tuning? After the first fine careless rapture is over, what level of sexual interest do you hope for?

The more detailed your definition, the fewer people are available to be guided to you. If you want to do a lot of interviewing, leave your definition wide. Remember: There will be many rejects and false starts. The finer and closer the definition, the more likely you are to get exactly what you want, with minimum waste motion. But—and it is a big but—you may have to wait a little longer. Don't be impatient.

You need to define all these things and lots more before you choose the picture or the psychic link that will serve as the center-piece of your ritual. So many chances for mismatch exist that you simply cannot afford to leave empty any of the blanks on the résumé of that target person.

To be worked out with someone who is seeking companionship, or to be done by the seeker him/herself. For personal or solitary use; rarely for group.

Type of Companionship Desired

Friendship   _____

Love   _____

Other   _____

Sexual Orientation   _____

Gender   _____

Height   _____

Weight   _____

Body Type   _____

Race   _____

Age (within a ten-year span)   _____

Years of College Completed   _____

Degree(s) Held   _____

Hobbies   _____

Areas of General Interest   _____

Employment   _____

Career   _____

Body Art (yes/no, location, type)   _____

Other   _____

Mind Keys

Sign	Emotion	Scent	Color	Touch	Taste	Sound

Psychic Links   _____

Work Sheet VIII-1
Companionship

WEALTH

MATERIALISM AND THE WEB

Sometimes it becomes difficult to understand how a ritual for wealth works. There may be surprises. In many cases a *person* is involved as the means to the end. A gentleman we know got a check from Blue Cross—though he was not a member. Being in dire need, he spent it. Notice that the check had to be approved and issued by some *person* in the Blue Cross hierarchy.

Another lady was gifted an almost-new car. Again, her boss—and it turns out, his girlfriend, who hated the car—were the intermediaries. Hence when you do a ritual for a physical object, you need to think of the actors in the drama who will gift you with your desire.

Sometimes, as in the fall of lottery balls, there is minimal human intervention. In such cases it is best to attempt to influence the balls directly as they fall. A woman of our acquaintance had some minor successes by pointing an amulet at the TV as the local lottery draw happened. (No, she wouldn't tell us how she made the amulet.)

DEFINING THE INTENT

As Work Sheet VIII-2 shows, you begin by defining the type of wealth, the immediate need, and some possible sources. In our earlier cautionary tale, the guy got money, but got downsized. At the age of 55, he found it very difficult to get new employment. It was not the best ritual in the world for his needs at that time. Remember then to specify the tradeoff you are prepared to make. Surely there always is one.

What are you willing to give up for an increase in wealth? Do you want a temporary surge of money, as you would get from winning a lottery, or do you want a continuous slight improvement? Be very careful of rituals that you design for bursts of money. One of the easiest ways to bring in a large amount abruptly is to have a traffic accident that results in an insurance payoff. Do you want to go through that sort of pain and inconvenience (to say nothing of the possible maiming and permanent disability you might bring on yourself)?

Type of Wealth Needed						
Immediate		$_____				
Raise		$_____				
Debt Reduction		$_____				
New Possession		_____				
Other		_____				
Possible Sources		_____				
Trade-off						
Loss of Job		_____				
Injury		_____				
Death of Relative		_____				
Relocation		_____				
Fire		_____				
Other		_____				
Possible Intermediaries		_____				
Mind Keys						
Sign	Emotion	Scent	Color	Touch	Taste	Sound

Work Sheet VIII-2
Wealth

The underlying question is whether the relentless omnipresence of today's advertising has pressured you into *believing* you need the latest and best Razzmobile/muscle car/SUV/Go-Devil just because they've got them to sell.

Should you in fact improve the quality of your life in other directions that are not so money-dependent? Over and over, when we counsel families in which the wife is working and the husband has a job and a half or even two jobs, we find that every family member (especially the kids) wants to spend more time with the parents. This may seem to go against the popular assumption that teenagers are not interested in listening to or being with their parents, but it is true. More time equates to a better quality of life for the whole family, even if they can't eat out all the time or have all the fashionable designer attire and electronic gadgets their peers may display and advertisers insist they need. Then eating out becomes an occasion, not something they have to do by default because no one has time to plan or cook meals.

As you complete the work sheet, we hope that you will answer these peripheral questions and settle on the best parameters for your ritual.

Health

The Karma of Healing

Wiccans pride themselves on their ethical rule:

If it harm none, do what you will.

When it comes to healing, some argue that the patient is learning a lesson through the disease, and that, if you cure him, that lesson will have to be repeated. That may be true in rare cases; but to us it sounds like simply an excuse not to try. Surely we are humans with sympathy and understanding. If we could save a child's life by simply stretching out a hand, we would automatically do it. Yet in such a case we might be really screwing with a child's karma. In the great scheme of things, it might be time for the child to progress.

So what is the answer? You must use your own best judgment in each case and add to your affirmation the idea:

If this is not the best use of the power, Guides and Elder Ones, use it as You see fit.

Defining the Healing Intents

Doctors are beginning to believe that the mind is the major factor in curing and healing of all disease. Although a Witch uses herbal and dietary cures in working for a healing, it is the *mind* of the patient that will be changed. Time and again in our cautionary tales we find that when one disease is cured, another takes its place. Illness can be a prize tool for manipulating the people around you, and there are individuals who feel (consciously or unconsciously) they are home free once they develop a complaint that lets them pull other people's strings. Clinging to a disease is the clearest possible indication that the patient *needs* the disease for his or her own reasons. Before you even consider a patient as a candidate for healing, make sure they have seen a regular doctor and you have seen what course of treatment the establishment recommends.

Name of Patient	
Patient's Age	
Patient's Religious Affiliation	
Physician's Diagnosis	
Apparent Disease	
Underlying Possibilities	
Relationships	
Job	
Environment	
Other	

Mind Keys for Ritual for Underlying Problem

Sign	Emotion	Scent	Color	Touch	Taste	Sound

| Psychic Links for Underlying Problem | |
| Mind Keys for Ritual for Apparent Disease | |

Sign	Emotion	Scent	Color	Touch	Taste	Sound

Psychic Links for Apparent Disease

Work Sheet VIII-3
Healing

Thus in thinking about a healing ritual, a great deal of effort must go into identifying the factor(s) in the patient's life circumstances that need to be changed, as well as working for the healing of the present disease.

This is not a simple matter. If someone asks you to work for a healing on a patient whom you know only slightly (or not at all), reject that request. Yes, such a ritual may sometimes work; but it is also true that these people usually get sick with some other ailment. Do a tarot reading for the patient. Use all your abilities to determine the underlying cause of the illness, and do a ritual for *that*, as well as for the surface disease. Work Sheet VIII-3 should help you define your ritual.

Another question comes to mind here, too. Why doesn't the patient himself ask for help? Surely the seeker has not gone *behind his back*? That possibility is simply too ugly to contemplate.

PROTECTION

In this most bigoted world, Witches and other people having "different" world views are often hated and feared. (*Different* and *Dangerous* both start with D, so people seem to make them interchangeable.) Over the years, then, Witches have developed psychic means to create adequate protection for themselves, their friends, and their property.

Protection of your dwelling while you sleep is usually all that is necessary, but occasionally you need more protection than the psychic sphere you can place around an abode. Then it is time to reinforce your basic protection with a personal amulet that you have made and charged in a ritual.[1] Occasionally, even this protection will be insufficient to afford the serenity you need; in these extreme cases you will want to protect each body orifice, so that absolutely nothing can affect you. All these protective systems are well known and have been practiced by Witches around the world since prehistoric times.

HAVE YOU BEEN HEXED?

Many people ask us how to distinguish signs of genuine psychic attack from the run of bad luck that can occasionally happen to anyone. The key to differentiating between the two is in the messages

---

[1]The best amulet procedure that we know of can be found in Chapter XI of our book, *The Witch's Magical Handbook*.

you receive during channeling. Sudden changes in your normal pattern of reception during meditation, disruption of the answers that you would normally get, and heavy negative feelings, when coupled with bad luck in your mundane life, are sure signs of psychic attack. No genuine psychic attack is without these indications. This is one of the reasons you should (a) become proficient in channeling and (b) channel every single day of your life.

Understanding the Forces Against You

Forces that operate on you are in the physical, "real" world and are what we refer to as *mundane* forces. They are not, as many believe, supernatural. They are certainly not manifestations of the devil—unless that devil is the person who is attacking you. The same force that you felt tickle the palm in your power-measurement experiments is the force that people will attempt to use against you. Everyone who has a pulse in their wrist has this power.

Some people naturally put out a great deal of it. Such people are sometimes called healers and at other times *Hexe* or *curanderos*. Names vary from ethnic group to ethnic group. Some people put it out deliberately, but many people have no control of their output. They may even be unaware of it. We have helped many people get their power into control. One lady who lived near us had the power to kill chickens. She hated them, because in childhood she had unwillingly been assigned to look after a large flock. Many people (especially Aries women, it seems) have the power to start fires. Of course this can be very dangerous.

Fortunately most of the powers you will be combating are poorly directed and controlled. For example, they might be powers proceeding from some neighbor who is temporarily angry at you. That hate may in fact send much negative energy in your direction; but it is easily reflected, for it has no real direction or control. Further, if she *is* aware of her power, she probably does not know effective ways to focus it.

Your Protective Mirror

Since time immemorial, mirrors and polished surfaces have been used with appropriate charming to reflect back the harmful intent of ill wishers and casters of the evil eye. Plastic mirrors are not as effective as heavy glass silvered mirrors, though reflective bronze and stainless steel seem to work well. A mirror by itself is inert and neutral. To make it work for you, place a picture of yourself behind the mirror as shown in Figure VIII-1. Then use an appropriate charming chant to activate the mirror-picture defensive combination:

Mirror, Mirror, work for me.
From slings and arrows keep me free.
As I will, so let it be.

Hold the mirror before your heart with its shining face outward as you face each of the six directions. Repeat the chant a total of six times. When that procedure is complete, it is a good idea to use this final affirmation:

Sphere of Magic, come with me.
Where'er I go, follow me.

Reinforce this protective ritual once every five days until the danger is past. If you can place the mirror with the picture behind it where the attacker can see it, this is the best possible defense. If you cannot arrange that, bury the mirror (face up) in dry sand to which you have added a little sulfur and salt.

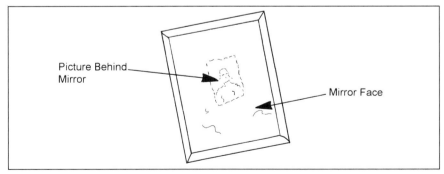

Figure VIII-1 — Your Mirror of Protection
(Picture is entirely hidden behind mirror.)

Bill, Sam, and the New Freeway

Bill and Sam are aldermen in a small town in eastern North Carolina. Often they find themselves on opposite sides of questions affecting the town's future. By and large Bill resists any scheme that would change the town in a way that would attract tourists to it. He represents the old-line "Let's keep it as it is" viewpoint. Sam, on the other hand, is eager to see the downtown area developed to its "full potential." He would like to see the waterfront lined with junk-food shacks and Las Vegas-style neon signs.

Never were their differences so clearly seen as when the state government decided to build a new freeway that would let traffic flow more smoothly to a nearby beach area. Bill and his friends wanted the freeway to bypass the town altogether; Sam and his party wanted it to go straight through downtown. The state government had no great tendency toward one route or the other; the routes were equal in desirability and cost. Therefore the state decided they would let the board of aldermen decide which route they liked better. Sam could see that the aldermen generally favored the bypass route, and was furious at the loss of revenue that he was sure downtown would suffer from the decision.

We were close friends with Bill. He told us one night that the downtown route had nearly been adopted at the last aldermanic meeting because many of the aldermen who favored the bypass route were mysteriously ill and unable to attend the meeting. He himself admitted to feeling unwell; nothing particularly significant, just headachy, but in spite of this he had most fortunately decided to go to the meeting. Sam proposed that the aldermen adopt the downtown route, and it would have passed, but Bill had been able to delay the vote until the next meeting. Bill was very worried that four or five of the aldermen were still apparently under the weather; their respective physicians had no idea what was wrong with them.

We had heard a rumor, that a local satanic group had decided they wanted the downtown route to win because they anticipated profiting from a large influx of tourists. They believed they could gain recruits from the tourist traffic through the use of psychic control and pushing illegal drugs. When we heard Bill's story of mysterious illness, we were fairly certain that these satanists had done a ritual to affect the aldermen.

After some hesitation, we decided to come clean and tell Bill what we suspected. Somewhat to our surprise, he did not laugh at our suspicions. We suggested that he let us protect his home and see whether he felt better afterward. If he did, he agreed that we should then protect the homes of a couple of the other aldermen who were his close friends and who would not be likely to object to such an unorthodox procedure.

The protection worked. The protection of the homes of three other aldermen also worked—to such an extent that the satanic group's negative ritual backfired on them. The bounced-off energy scattered the group. Today the bypass stands as silent evidence of the victory won by Bill and his allies; the town still drowses in its friendly, slow-paced backwater.

YOUR GODS OF THE SIX DIRECTIONS

You should protect yourself against people who may, either deliberately or inadvertently, send negative energies against you. Even if you don't want to teach them a lesson by returning those energies to them, you still should not add to their egos by letting them think they have harmed you. You can easily arrange to be above all that and immune to it.

To help people protect themselves, European magicians developed the symbol shown in Figure VIII-2. It is called the symbol of the Gods of the Six Directions. Make this for yourself as a protection for your home. To fully activate the protection, obtain a piece of parchment-like paper. On it reproduce the symbol in Figure VIII-2. Hang this on the wall opposite the foot of your bed. Now get six mirror tiles, each 12 inches square. On each one reproduce, with waxy crayon, one of the six sigils shown in the various directions in the figure. Place each mirror with shiny side outward

around your home in its proper direction so you are totally surrounded by a sphere of protection. As you place each one, say the
appropriate incantation from Table VIII-1 to charge that sigil with
its full protective power. Start with the one that belongs in the attic
representing "above."

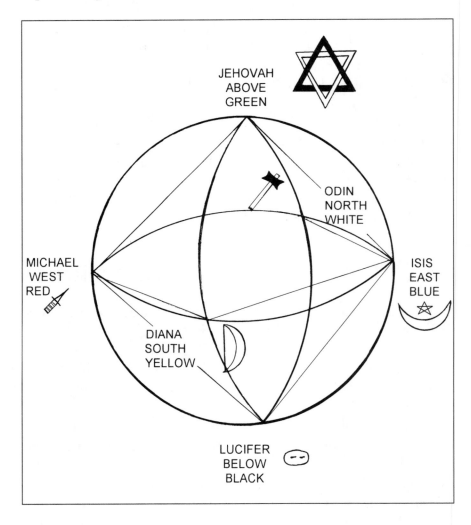

Figure VIII-2
Symbols and Colors of the
Gods of Six Directions

Direction	Deity	Incantation
East	Isis	Goddess of the flowing Nile, Rise in east; shield me the while. Energize the dawn for me. As I will, so let it be.
South	Diana	Fecund goddess of the sun, Guard me while my life does run. Energize the day for me. As I will, so let it be.
West	Michael	Mighty archangel of the west, As the day closes, secure my rest. Energize the west for me. As I will, so let it be.
North	Odin	Odin, mighty god of the north, Bring wisdom and safety to me forth. Energize the night for me. As I will, so let it be.
Above (attic)	Jehovah	Come from your overseeing chair With mighty power everywhere. Energize the sky for me. As I will, so let it be.
Below (basement)	Lucifer	Light-Bearer, come with mighty power; Shield me in every perilous hour. Energize the earth for me. As I will, so let it be.
Gods of the east, south, west, and north: Protect me as I work and play, God above and god below, Protect me all the night and day.		

Table VIII-1
*Incantations to Charge and Reinforce the Gods of the Six Directions
and Your Sphere of Protection*

Yes, your attic may be dusty. Sometimes the crawl space under the house is dirty too. Once the sigils are situated, they do not need to be replaced. You renew them this way: Every time you go to bed or get up, think in a positive way of a blue-white-gold sphere of protection surrounding your house. Each evening, sit in bed, look at your symbol, and repeat the six incantations from Table VIII-1. This ensures that your sphere will be reinforced anew and nothing can pierce it while you sleep or during the next day.

Why call on the names of the various deities? They personify the energies you are trying to use. Their names indicate the great cosmic pools of power which you are tapping into for your defense. If you like, they are *mind keys* through which you call up the energies you need. You are not summoning the actual deities; you are summoning energies tuned to their vibratory level.

Your Psychic Second Line of Defense

The protection that we arranged for the aldermen against the satanic group by using the Gods of the Six Directions was quick and efficient. Our task was easier because the satanic group had not directed all its energies against one individual target but had worked a shotgun effort. When energy is scattered in that way, the Gods of the Six Directions constitute an extremely efficient shield; however, when energy *is* focused and directed, you need a better shield than this outer sphere of protection affords. At such a time you will want to draw the sphere in closer to you and reinforce the body's natural protection with some physical devices.

If detectable disturbances still occur in your channeling, that means that your house protection and even your personalized mirror protection are not adequate. Now is the time to develop those defensive devices or talismans that are the final line, the ultimate in psychic defense, used by competent occultists for centuries.

Talismans to Guard the Holes in Your Defense

Talismans worn on the body are your ultimate line of defense. When a powerful and directed psychic attack manifests itself, you must use strong measures to reflect it. It must not get into your body. As you know, the body has several apertures or orifices, both psychic and mundane. Each orifice should be protected with a mirror talisman or other easily constructed defensive device. Reviewing the various areas:

PROTECTING THE BRAIN AND THE HEAD

Psychic energies can directly influence the brain. It appears that the majority of these energies flow in through the *third eye*. This is the site in the center of the forehead which high-caste Hindus protect with the red caste mark. Some people, like Native Americans and the younger more "turned-on" generation, wear leather headbands with appropriate protective devices beaded into them. Natural leather by itself is an excellent protective material; somehow it stops the flow of psychic energy. A leather skullcap in the shape of the yarmulke worn by Jewish men makes an excellent protector for the back of the head.

For total protection, the head needs more than even leather provides. Many centuries ago it was found that an iron band placed around the forehead forms a total protective circle. Because of this, members of our own groups have relied for years on leather-bound iron bands placed in hat brims as a complete protective device for both the third eye and the brain. Figure VIII-3 shows how to make such a device. Your local craft store will have available both the wire and the natural leather you need to make it.

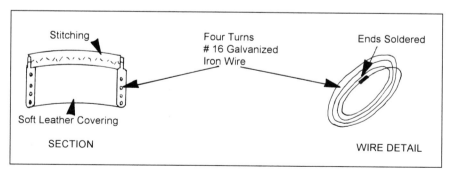

Figure VIII-3
Your Protective Headband
(Wear under hat.)

Salves like lipstick, eye shadow,[2] or plain petroleum jelly can be charmed and used as protection for eyes, mouth, and nose. Most women selecting jewelry for the ears do not take sufficient care, when they could choose something useful.

PROTECTING THE HEART AND THE THROAT

Protective jewelry should always be of steel or silver. It should have bright, shiny surfaces, should bear protective sigils, and should be properly charmed.

The simplest protective talisman you can use is a necklace. There are many most powerful protective engravings you can put on a medallion hung so that it lies precisely between the nipples. The larger and flatter and more highly polished is the outer surface of this medallion, the better protection it will afford. Like other protective tamulets, heart-protecting talismans should be of steel and highly polished. A smaller version of the heart talisman should be worn on a choker to protect the throat.

THE HANDS

Protecting the hands is a matter of selecting the correct rings for the ring finger of your receiving hand. Very small amounts of energy flow either out of or into the other fingers.[3]

A typical example of sigilation for a protective ring for an Aries woman is shown in Figure VIII-4. The horns point outward; the

Figure VIII-4
Ring of Protection—Example

---

[2]People in many eastern countries wear black kohl eye liner to ward off the evil eye. Reflective silver or gold eye liner seems to work best.

[3]Protective rings are available from Godolphin House, P.O. Box 297-B, Hinton WV 25951, and on the web at www.wicca.org.

birth sign points inward toward the body of the wearer. The pentagram to give her continuous good health points inward. If you desire
it, you can also wear a closed steel ring on your wrist; this must be
welded shut to form a continuous circle of metal.

YOUR PSYCHIC CHASTITY BELT

In past centuries, talismans to cover the genital area were also made
of steel. Undergarments embroidered with symbols taken from
Appendix One, Table 2, and powerfully charged now serve this purpose. Washing such garments removes the efficacy of the charm, so
you will need to recharm them after laundering.

PROTECTING YOUR FEET

The feet are the simplest body part to protect, but are often overlooked as an area needing protection. An anklet can stop the flow of
negative energy from the ground. If you look at native peoples who
regularly go barefoot, you will see that they wear a multiplicity of
anklets and ankle adornments. All these are designed to prevent psychic energy from coming in through this unprotected avenue. You
should follow their example now that you no longer wear leather on
your feet. (Today's technology has removed the natural leather that
previously offered psychic protection to the feet, replacing the
leather with synthetic materials.) Even the most sophisticated
occultists often neglect to protect their feet at night. They scrupulously wear shoes only of natural leather—but fail to wear anklet
protection while in bed.

PROTECTING YOUR NAVEL

Finally in your armory of protective devices, you must have a tamulet
to shield the navel, which after all is the original pathway of the life
force into your body. A large and ornate belt buckle is the simplest
way to ensure such protection. This too should be highly polished,
properly sigilated and charmed, and worn constantly. The navel can
be covered with appropriate embroidery placed on a garment, but it
is more usual to wear a properly designed belt buckle for this purpose. Your navel should be protected at all times, just like every other

vulnerable part of your body, whether you believe you are under psychic attack or not. Many occultists work at night when they believe you may be careless or off-guard about arranging your defenses.

Attack: The Best Form of Defense

The people who are likely to attack you psychically have one failing in common; it is the chink in their psychic armor that you can so easily use to beat them at their own game. That chink is their ego. For some reason, just like mundane-world criminals, they feel they know more and are cleverer than anyone else. Time and again we find this attitude in people who run two-bit occult groups and so-called covens, groups usually limited to a handful of sick, sycophantic hangers-on. These hangers-on feed the ego of the self-styled sorcerer or "queen." The mirrors we have been recommending reflect back the energy they send; this will usually wipe them out, there is no need for an overt attack.

Protecting All Phases of Your Life

We have discussed three spheres of protection:

1. The Sphere That Protects Your Dwelling Place (the Gods of Six Directions)

This sphere should always be in place, for you never know when someone will ill-wish you. Realize that it is not a totally protective sphere. If someone brings a negative amulet within the sphere, it will not protect you. Also, it does not travel with you; it is limited to the time when you are within your house.

2. Your Personalized Mirror-Protection

This is more powerful and more personal than the sphere installed around your dwelling. It protects you in the Six Directions and reinforces your home sphere of protection by forming a sphere within a sphere.

3. Protection of Body Orifices

Normally dwelling and mirror protections are all you will need, even if you have incurred the wrath of a neighbor or a local small occult group. However, if it is the wrath of a trained occultist, no matter how stupid you think him, do not fall into the same ego trap that catches him. He can harm you, and he will try. To protect yourself thoroughly against negative power sent to damage you, you must wear talismans on your body to protect all its orifices and to reflect back the negative energies aimed at you. It is even more important to wear talismans during the night than during the day, for it is at night that most of these occultists work their negative magic.

God Talks to George

There's an old story about the man marooned on a rooftop during a flood on the Mississippi River. Let's call him George. George prayed hard to be rescued. Sure enough, a local fisherman, a friend of George's, arrived. George waved him off. "God will provide!" The next day a huge barge washed against the house; George could easily have stepped aboard. He didn't; "God will provide!" The next day, when the water had risen to a truly dangerous height, a National Guard helicopter crew offered a ride. No way was George going to give up now.

George drowned. When he got to heaven, he asked Jehovah why he hadn't saved him. Jehovah replied (expletives deleted): "I sent you a friend, a barge, and a helicopter, George! What more did you want?"

In another story, a similar George prayed for years to win the lottery. In heaven Jehovah's reply was, "Next time buy a ticket!"

Buy a Ticket

Do not overlook the obvious and simple solutions:

1. If you want a new companion, go to places that likely candidates frequent. Take classes in subjects that you enjoy. Go ballroom dancing. Go to the motocross or to the meeting of the local ecology society.

2. If you want to do a healing or be healed yourself, first enroll in an EMT course or a Red Cross course. Learn all you can about the disease in question. Even here there may be a simple solution.

3. Before you try to influence the fall of the numbered lottery balls, *buy a ticket*.

4. Channeling will tell you whether you need psychic protection. So:

   a. channel every day, and
   b. if you need protection—do it.

CHAPTER NINE

GETTING YOUR DUCKS IN A ROW

RAISING AND DIRECTING POWER[1]

There are several well-known ways to raise power; that is, to bring your output of energy, and the group's, to a maximum and then send that energy out to its target. The methods we have recommended in the past include:

1. Dance lightly clad or sky-clad with someone of the opposite psychic gender. Alternating fast clockwise dances and slow spins around the Circle are best, changing partners after every slow spin. Key the type and tempo of the music to the intent.[2] As the dance ends, all the participants join hands, step rapidly toward the center, and raise their clasped hands. They release hands and scream out the intent.

---

[1] We recommend you read our two companion books to this text: *The Magic Power of White Witchcraft* and *The Witch's Magical Handbook*. Pay particular attention to Chapter III of *The Witch's Magical Handbook*.

[2] See Table 4 in Appendix One.

2. Chant. Start the chant quietly in the low bass region and build it up in volume and pitch until you scream out the intent at the end. The actual chant should be a simple multiple repetition of a simple sound.[3] (Breathe at will.)

3. Charge an article (perhaps a god/ess figurine) with your intent. At the peak of your effort, drop the article into boiling water or into the fire. You can temporarily discharge crystals and natural material objects in the same way.

4. Invite the power of old god/esses to help. In no case do we recommend calling these forces *into* your protective Circle; especially *never* invite them to possess anyone. Well-trained Santería practitioners seem able to do this safely and to get rid of the possession, but we have never met a western Witch or pagan who has done it successfully and come away undamaged. In German practice the god/ess is called into a *vril eck* at a safe distance from the main circle; this practice can be safe and effective.[4]

Your God Bargain

A part of any ritual (though one that seems to have fallen out of favor) is the god bargain. You may already have entered into god bargains when a situation seemed to be out of hand; Christians especially are prone to say something like, "Jesus, if you get me out of this one, I'll go to church every Sunday for a year." From artifacts, we know that in ancient times the god bargain was common practice. For example, the cenotes of Mexico are full of beautifully made—but broken—artifacts, and social anthropologists tell us that the Druids did the same thing, both with artifacts and with agricultural products.

Table IX-1 lists typical examples of god/esses keyed to intents. Choose a deity for the intent at hand, from your own ethnic background: one that you are comfortable with.

---

[3]Appendix One, Table 4.
[4]Frost and Frost, *Power Secrets from a Sorcerer's Private Magnum Arcanum* (Godolphin House).

Intent	Norse	Irish	Egyptian	Greco-Roman	Christian	Yours
Desire	Loki	Nuada	Osiris	Scorpio	Lucifer	
Wealth	Vidar	Danu	Ra	Ceres	Mary	
Love	Freya	Branwen	Hathor	Aphrodite	Adonai	
Serenity	Heimdal	Cernunnos	Isis	Neptune	Jonah	
Healing*	Frigga	Bridget	Imhotep	Aries	Asclepius	
Attack	Thor	Cuchulain	Horus	Mars	Michael	
Luck	Fulla	Gwydion	Neith	Jupiter	Azazael	
Protection	Odin	Dagda	Anubis	Ceres	Raphael	

*General healing; depends on illness.

Table IX-1
God/esses for Seven Intents

Before a ritual begins, write a note to the chosen deity stating what you are willing to do or to give up if the ritual is successful. The sacrifice has to be something of real value to you. You might want to follow the old example and make some beautiful object to be broken at the height of the ritual or you might want to give up something that would provide pleasure. Then the god bargain can be, "We forgo our pleasure for the sake of _____."

Constructing Your Ritual Space

Once you have decided on a location, you can move ahead and construct a work area within it. There are two types of area you need.

1. A *container* sphere to contain power until you send it out to your target.
2. A psychically *protected* sphere in which to channel.

These spheres are represented by circles cast on the ground or on your work surface. Always construct your circle to the size of the sacred Measure. Table IX-2 shows how the dimensions for the outer protective circle and the containment circle vary.

Type of Circle	Size-Megalithic Yards Diameter	Size-Feet* Diameter
Table Top	1	2.72
Personal	2	5.44
Small Group (2–12)	4	10.88
Large Group (12–56)	8	21.76

*These dimensions are in decimals of a foot. 2.72 = 2 feet, 8⁴¹⁄₆₄ inches.

Table IX-2
Circle Sizes

Interestingly enough, these radii give a circle whose mini-divisors total seventeen units. This means that if you mark off the circumference with a one-foot measuring stick, the circle will divide into seventeen units. Seventeen is a prime number—indivisible; so this circlet is ideal as a protective device. Remember: Only those circles made of electrically conducting materials will work. Typical effective materials are:

1. Damp sea salt[5]
2. Copper wire ¼-inch in diameter
3. Charcoal
4. Copper sulfate
5. Burnt sulfur

Your Circle of Containment

When you plan only to put out energy, you need only one circle to contain the energy before you send it out. This circle can be as small as your altar top, where it contains energy from (for instance) a candle ritual. Or as large as necessary to contain a group. In such a circle you may use small amounts of magnetic materials, perhaps the rod in your wand. Do not use any closed rings. Remember to remove such things as your protective finger ring.

Your Circle of Protection

Traditionally circles of protection protect against mundane energy from living people and energy from god/esses and other non-human

---

[5]May be colored to fit the intent.

sources. To do these two protections adequately, you will draw two more circles inside your containment circle. The mini-divisors of one will total sixteen; the mini-divisors of the innermost will total fifteen. Sixteen is a number associated with the earth plane, and fifteen is of the psychic plane. When you have circles cast in this way, you can use the divisors to do such things as draw a five-pointed star in the inner circle. Table IX-3 shows the dimensions of the inner circles.

Type	Outer Diameter	Second Diameter	Inner Diameter
Personal	5.44	5.12	4.8
Small Group	10.88	10.24	9.6
Large Group	21.76	20.48	19.2

Table IX-3
Dimensions in Feet for Inner Circles

Between the outer two circles it is usual to place herbs appropriate to the intent. Between the two innermost circles, workers draw signs of the zodiac and place burning candles and bowls of water. Figure IX-1 shows how your circle might look at this stage.

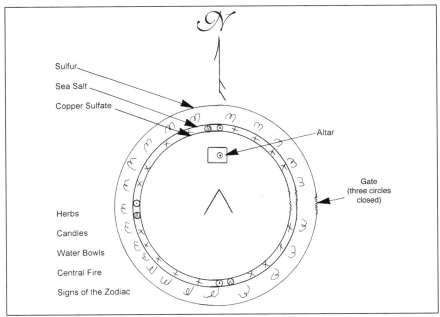

Figure IX-1 — Ritual Circle

The illustration includes an altar placed in the north. The altar need be present only for large group rituals. In smaller rituals the tools are placed on the hearth. The eastern gate will be closed during the ritual. Usually only the outer gate is closed for the first part and all three gates are closed for the channeling section that occurs when the participants return after grounding.

YOUR HOLY SPACE

The circle you have constructed represents a sacred space. If you think about it, you will see that as you enter the eastern gate you cross from outer darkness through the earth plane, then through the planet plane, and into the spiritual plane. The central stone hearth and its fire represent either the earth and the heavens (ascending fumes) or your body (stone) and your spirit (fire).

STEPS BEYOND

The mathematical work we describe just here is optional. If you have a mathematical or experimental turn of mind, you might like to take some additional steps in the construction of your sacred space. The Ancients built their structures in *earth-commensurate* measure; that is to say, they measured a degree of latitude near the ritual location and then divided that figure by the length of the year in days. This resulted in their basic foot—their *unit*. Countless old buildings are built to dimensions based on this unit. Of course when the length of the year changed, the Measure changed with it. Thus the British foot—far from being some arbitrary or whimsical measure—is precisely 1/365,242.198 times a degree of latitude at Stonehenge. Why did they do it? *How* did they do it? We don't really know. You will find, though, that if you take the time and trouble to construct circles using the correct celestially tuned Measure, your results will suddenly show an improvement.

To find your earth-commensurate foot, take a degree of latitude at your site in feet; divide it by 365,242.198.[6] The result is your "foot." Your foot multiplied by 2.72 is your megalithic yard.

It is appropriate to note the lengths to which the Ancients went to make sure that their constructions were accurate, both symbolically and mathematically. Buildings from the great pyramid to Greek temples to the thousands of stone circles in Europe were all built to the Measure. Trained people used the Measure from prehistoric times up through medieval churches and cathedrals. Glastonbury Cathedral, for example, is noted for its use of 2.72 and for its nave floor area of 666 astronomic square feet. The nave pavement is 9 MY × 10 MY because: $2.72 \times 2.72 \times 9 \times 10 = 666$.

The Golden Section is the proportion manifested in a spiral form such as the shell of a snail, and it is also the measure most instinctively pleasing to the eye. In modern times Frank Lloyd Wright used it in many of his buildings. The United Nations Building in New York City is built on a golden section. The relationship between the *Golden Section* (1.618) and the *Megalithic Yard* (2.72) is inherent in the legs of a Pentagram which are all golden sections.

Now you have combined three things in your triple circle:

1. A measure that tunes it to the earth

2. An arrangement that connects the Golden Section to the Megalithic Yard

3. A sacred-space symbology shared with all ancient cathedrals and churches. (The nave=mundane. The area past the altar rail=heavenly. The area behind the altar [the holy of holies]=spiritual.)

The Church of Wicca has taken a further experimental step in investigating the use of the *oval*. The ancient stone circles were all built to what is called the cosmic egg shape, a very slight oval. Recently we have started constructing "circles" as shown in Figure IX-2. They do work better, especially when you have male and female

---

[6] *Compton's Encyclopedia* (both in paper and on disk) has a table of degree sizes in miles. Convert by multiplying by 5,280.

leaders, because each leader has a focal point to work from. This construct gives up the possibility of the central pentagram construction and thus has not found favor; no matter that it works better.

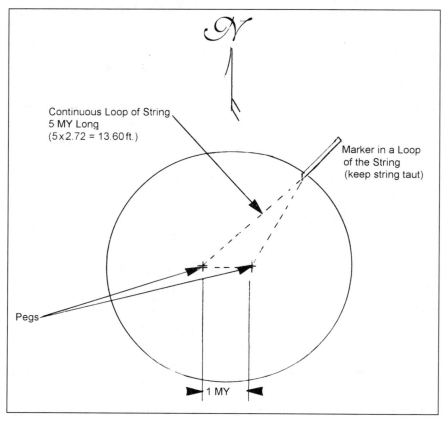

Figure IX-2
Constructing the Cosmic Egg

YOUR RITUAL FLOW

All rituals that work properly flow in the same way and follow the same foundation sequence. It breaks simply into five main parts.

1. Prepare:

    a. Define the intent and establish timing.

    b. Get mind keys.

    c. Get psychic links.

    d. Secure location.

    e. Prepare location.

    f. Secure cooperation of other participants (train if necessary).

    g. Fast.

    h. Become celibate (if "sex" magic is involved).

2. Recharge yourself.

3. Raise power:

    a. Cast circles.

    b. Complete the setup.

    c. Bring in participants.

    d. Close outer circle.

    e. Raise power.

    f. Send it out.

    g. Use any power remaining in circle.

    h. Open circle.

4. Channeling:

    a. Ground.

    b. Return to circle.

    c. Close and seal all circles.

    d. Welcome and honor god/esses.

    e. Bless bread and wine.

    f. Pass bread and wine.

    g. Channel.

    h. Report experiences.

    i. Open circles.

5. Feast and follow up:

    a. Clean up circles and dispose of used materials.

    b. Have a good group meal.

    c. Discuss possible meanings for the channeling results.

    d. Over the next three months have everyone keep a diary of results.

Figure IX-3 shows how the psychic output of participants typ-ically changes during the sequence of events before, during, and after a ritual. You can see that to change the order will cause problems; for instance, if you try to channel at the beginning when everyone is up, you are unlikely to get good results.

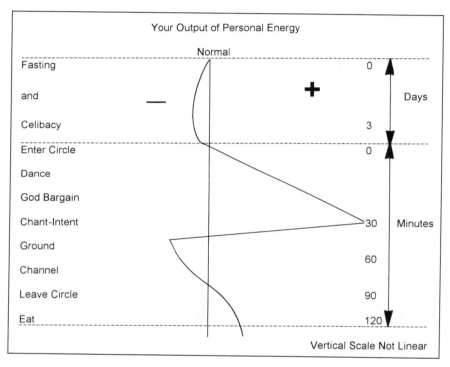

Figure IX-3
Levels of Excitement versus Ritual Sequence

Your Ritual Work Sheets

Work Sheets IX-1 and IX-2 are designed both to help you make sure you haven't overlooked anything and to help you establish that you can in fact be ready on the date proposed for the ritual. From these tables you will construct the all-important Ritual Action, Planning, and Timing (RAPT) chart.

Days to Acquire/Do				Notes
Item or Task	**Have**	**Minimum**	**Maximum**	
Altar				
Robe				
Athame				
Book of Light				
Chalice				
Bowls				
Mead or Wine				
Candles				
Matches				
Candle Holders				
Charcoal				
Herbs				
Flasks				
Spring or Rain Water				
Tape Deck				
Music Tape				
Sea or Kosher Salt				
Sulfur				
Copper Sulfate				

Work Sheet IX-1
Your Materials Check Chart

Days to Acquire/Do				Notes
Item or Task	Have	Minimum	Maximum	
Intent				
Timing				
Mind Keys				
Psychic Links				
Location Contract				
Prepare Location				
Participants				
Training Participants				
Prepare Dance Music Tape				
Dye Robe				
Fast and Celibacy				
Go to Location				

Work Sheet IX-2
Your Task Check Chart

Copy these charts. Use them as an *aide-memoir* and checklist to make sure that you have all the pieces necessary to complete the ritual.

Longest Path, Shortest Time

Work Sheets IX-1 and IX-2 ask you to enter minimum and maximum time, in days, for each item you will need in the ritual. Notice that many of these activities can be done in *parallel*. The intent can be defined, the location found, in parallel—in other words, in the same day or week. Until you define your intent, though, you cannot identify the mind keys or establish the base timing; so these are what we call *serial* applications. In general the items in Work Sheet IX-1 can be obtained or made in parallel with one another even well before you plan to do any specific ritual.

In Work Sheet IX-2 there is more dependence of one task on another. These are serial activities. Once you establish the intent, the mind keys, psychic links, and timing become parallel activities.

Your RAPT Chart

The Ritual Action, Planning, and Timing chart guides you to figure out both the longest and the shortest time in which you can prepare for your ritual. Figure IX-4 shows a small section of such a chart.

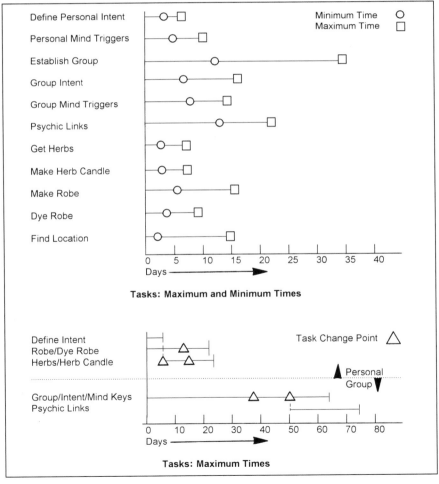

Figure IX-4
Section of Your RAPT Chart

Get a large sheet of squared (quadrille) paper and fill it in for yourself. For each item or task, draw a line representing both the minimum and maximum times. In the figure we have done this for Intent, for Mind Keys, and for Psychic Links. The figure shows that the Psychic-Link worst case will need the longest lead time.

When you fill in the number of days for the next task, it must back onto or add to (in our case) the Psychic-Link item. At first sight this may be confusing; but once you begin to work with it, you will see how it all locks together to give you the lead time that you should plan on for doing your ritual. Then you can review the timing, to see how it fits with the RAPT chart. You may have to come back and tighten up in certain areas—giving yourself less time to find a location, for instance.

This type of chart is common in industry where it serves in the development of new products. These are critical path charts that show the items that take longest to complete and when added together give the longest time for the development of a new product, such as your ritual.

Bobbie Jean Disqualifies Herself

Bobbie Jean Smithers lives in our own town of Hinton, West Virginia. Planning to do a healing ritual for a mental patient, we had contacted the proposed participants, who were all initiates of our path. Some of them had to drive long distances, and we had a house full the night before the ritual. During that evening Bobbie Jean called to say that she did not feel right about the ritual since she knew the man whom we planned to help and felt that he was just a malingering chip-on-the-shoulder, the-world-owes-me-a-living type—that we would be better off working a different ritual. Since we had all gathered, and since most of the members did not share Bobbie Jean's feelings, we went ahead with our plans.

Nothing seemed to happen to Richard, the target; if anything, his problems seemed to grow worse. At the same time his social worker seemed to toughen up her response to his whining. She told him to get out and get a job because she was going to cut him off.

After several weeks of misery, Richard did in fact get a job. Today he is a reasonable contributing member of the community.

Was Bobbie Jean right? Did the ritual affect the social worker instead of Richard? Who knows? The point is that Bobbie Jean felt she would detract from the ritual instead of adding to its effectiveness. She would be, if you like, a dead battery when it came to raising power—or, even worse, a very negative influence.

This Is Not a Democracy

In general, ritual groups run in a democratic manner. But when it comes to a ritual that has been agreed upon, the leader(s) must be dogmatic and dynamic. Any participant who feels as Bonnie Jean did should simply elect out with no blame. Ideally they won't leave it till the last minute as she did; but (s)he should be smart enough to realize that (s)he will take away from the ritual rather than add to it, and ethical enough to behave in an adult manner.

The basic Witch's ethic is summed up in a saying or *Rede*. It is:

If it harm none, do what you will.

The "none" includes yourself. The "harm" may be physical, mental, or psychic. When you look at an intent in a ritual, you may not interpret it the way another person will. A person may believe that a certain healing should not be done because the patient has the illness for a karmic reason—a learning experience. If the intent cannot be modified so that the participant is comfortable with it, let them elect out of the ritual.

In our path, we believe that the participants must be fully trained. We let people participate in our small *working* rituals only when they have been with us for a full year and a day, and have been initiated. In large group rituals, you will very often find that some of the participants are totally untrained while others are experts. Large rituals can be real grab-bags. Since you have so many people, though, the very quantity of raw energy seems to overcome the few negative or unskilled people. Again, the leader(s) must be dogmatic and dynamic. "This is what we are going to do. This is how we are going to do it. And we are going to do it at 11:35 this evening."[7] Anyone who doesn't wish to participate should leave.

Alternatives Are Okay

Inmates have reported excellent success rates when they perforce use *drawings* of tools and candles. These are mind keys, so you too can use alternatives. When you look at the RAPT Chart and your tables of necessary equipment, if something is missing, and getting it will mean a delay in the ritual, use a substitute. After all, it's really the intent and what is in your mind that will give the result, not the dogmatic following of every minute rule. The Guides know your level of sincerity and will work with you accordingly.

Nor should you worry if some of the words that you use are different from the words we suggest. Interestingly, Gavin attended a Wiccan circle in Sicily with people of several different nationalities. For this occasion, to avoid the Tower of Babel syndrome, the service was conducted *silently*. Gavin reports that they had two dramatic healing successes that night.

The Last Three Days of the World as You Knew It

If this is your first ritual, please, please do everything you possibly can to prepare for it and somehow take a vacation or get away for the three days preceding the actual day. Ideally you will spend this time in a relaxed, meditative environment, avoiding such things as news broadcasts, perhaps reading a couple of those books that have awaited your attention for so long. No electronics at all. Detach from the paycheck world and all its stresses.

---

[7]Stipulating a specific number of minutes tends to get people to attend on time; whereas they interpret "12 o'clock" to mean *something near 12 o'clock.*

Use these three days to review all the ritual preparations, even if you are not actually running the ritual. Ask the proposed leader(s) to work with you to review everything that will happen. There should be no secrets and no surprises; for secrets and surprises will ruin the mood of any ritual—and thus its effectiveness as well. When you are doing regular rituals, you may not have the freedom to take time off in this way; but at least for your first one, make it more meaningful, a time apart. Perhaps you should rent a room at a local hotel and just vegetate there. Isolation may be the only way to guarantee that your mood is calm and respectful, free of hassle. Sometimes the home environment will get in the way of detachment. Be respectful and committed to what you are doing, and the results will be much more productive and dramatic.

Throughout this book we have been saying that ritual not only causes something to happen Out There; it also wreaks interior changes on the participants. Once you have worked ritual, you will find, your world view shifts. Sometimes if you jump right back into your old life, the shift will be temporary; but for many of us it can be so dramatic that it means the old life is no longer comfortable and we have eventually to make changes in it. Those changes might be small—spring-cleaning all the negative associated things out of our life matrix—or they lead to major milestones—such dramatic steps as changing careers and even finding new companionship. Whatever the aftereffects of the ritual itself, your participation in it is likely to affect you in major ways.

At the School of Wicca we regularly initiate new Witches. Occasionally candidates come to circle in a carefree, light-hearted way. Or perhaps worse, they come with a know-it-all attitude. These poor souls may go away unaffected. We note in their folders, "Initiation didn't take." Fortunately, most of the neophytes we initiate are visibly changed. On a couple of occasions they have gone away on such a spiritual high that their aura is actually visible to cowans[8] whom they meet. A couple of times our new initiates have been asked, "Who are you? What's that I see around you? Are you

---

[8]A non-Craft person. As Greeks speak of barbarians, as Scots highlanders speak of sassenachs, so Wiccans speak of cowans.

electrically charged?" This to one of our initiates flying homeward, from a flight attendant who was concerned lest the initiate affect the plane's electronics.

Don't Panic

People seem to experience many and varied problems on the last day before a ritual. This happens so often that we believe there is some unconscious psychic reason for it. The bank calls, the kids get sick, the car won't start, and a thousand other things happen to our neophytes on their way (for example) to their initiatory ritual. Some people even have such events before their first meditation. Why this is, we don't know—but it may be that people are overly concerned that their reality will in fact tilt—either with meditation or in going through a ritual. If your reality is going to tilt, it will tilt anyway—if not in this ritual or this initiation, it will move gradually as you grow further in your occult (alternative) studies. Most people would rather have that tilt occur quickly and today rather than have it come back and bite them in a tender place later in life when their resilience and adaptability are lower and they are more resistant to change.

Expect things to come off the spool just a little. There's a saying: "If things can go wrong, they will." This is the day in your life when they will. If you expect things to go wrong, of course they will be more likely to go wrong. Try not to put energy into that negative thought pattern—but if something does go wrong, don't panic. Just carry right on. The preparation you have done so far has been designed to avoid all the obvious glitches that so many ritualists make. You have a ritual for your ritual. Following it will make sure that nothing goes wrong that cannot be quickly corrected.

CHAPTER TEN

THE MASTER RITUAL

TODAY'S THE DAY

All the things we've said about the last three days before a ritual are doubly important on the last day before the ritual—the eve of the occasion. There is no point in coming to a ritual all hassled up and grinding your teeth because you're ready to kill someone in the "real" world. You must come with a relaxed mind, free of worrying what e-mail messages you may have missed or why your pager isn't working. Yvonne will tell you that *for her,* using any electronics on that last day is a disaster. The final countdown to the circle must be in a spirit of reverence and gratitude.

To get into that state, we recommend that three or four hours before the time scheduled for the ritual, you take a long relaxing bath, maybe adding a little lavender to the water. You can use either lavender oil or lavender blossoms (contained in a net bag which you suspend under the hot-water faucet so the water will run through it as the bathtub fills). Before you bathe, do all the usual cosmetic grooming steps you would do on a normal day. When you have bathed and dried yourself, put on your clean robe and go to join the other coveners in quiet conversation and contemplation of the ritual intent. All too often we find rituals get badly deformed by people coming in hastily at the last minute who are not properly prepared, deformed by delays in such things as casting the circles, or deformed by conversations on inappropriate topics.

The actual casting of the circle puts many experienced workers automatically into the mood for the ritual. A British Witch once told Gavin, "When I hear the kettle whistle, I know it's time for tea and biscuits." It's an almost Pavlovian reaction. When the bell rings or the priestess calls the participants to the ritual with notes on a recorder, they automatically move into a different mind space—an alternate reality.

Remember Ritual Order

Every ritual should follow the standard ritual sequence, no matter the intent or how "big" the ritual is. To review:

Preparation

This may last several days. It includes:

1. the gathering together of participants and equipment, including mind keys and psychic links; and
2. the cleansing and preparation of the space where you will work.

The Ritual

The ritual includes:

1. the raising of energy;
2. the use of mind keys to tune participants to the intent;
3. the psychic links to the target, and the screaming-out of the intent;
4. the grounding, and the channeling.

FOLLOW UP

You should follow up both immediately after the channeling effort, and over several days afterward.

You can consider the first part of the standard ritual format to be a *magical* procedure dealing with the mundane world. The second part, after grounding, is a *spiritual* procedure dealing with the "occult" (non-physical, *hidden*) world. You can see how the grounding and the adjustment of body chemistry takes you from the excitement and arousal of the dance and the chant into the relaxed meditative state necessary for channeling and journeying. Be clear in your mind about the distinction between these two aspects of ritual working, and make sure you do the appropriate steps in each section.

THE MASTER RITUAL FORMAT

You can change the words that you use in a ritual to those that are more pleasing to the group. In the ritual given below, remember that in every affirmation the words *or similar* are implied. Express each affirmation in your own words, and let the group recommend changes. This way the ritual is tuned to you and your group, and no one will silently harbor mental reservations that will kill your effectiveness.

You should not change the *sequence* of the steps in the ritual. The ritual words, the psychic links, the mind keys, and the elements: with care all can be changed to suit your ritual purpose. Then the format can be modified for rituals

1. to change the mundane future to be more to your liking;

2. for spiritual reasons, to contact Those Above with your message;

3. to honor the seasons or something similar—just because it's time for This One;

4. for someone who has gone on—who has graduated in "death";
   a. tell them they're released and should go on.
   b. get workers themselves back in tune after that departure.

    c. forgiveness (of graduate and/or self), to help release the graduate and to release those who are left behind from the attention of the graduate.

5. to form a group feeling or group mind: "We're all in this together";

6. and an infinity of other intents we have not named.

Remember the mood of ritual. Underneath, all rituals should be serious. This seriousness can be tempered so that the ritual can be gentle, easy, uplifting, intense, merry, whatever is appropriate. But when you call on the Elder Ones, or the Directions, or the Elements, you had better be respectful.

Sometimes leaders conduct what we call warm fuzzy rituals just to make the participants feel good. In such a case, the following ritual format might be considered too serious. As ever, respectfully adapt to fit the group and the occasion.

Time for Ritual

After the circles are cast, and when the central fire or charcoal is burning, one of the leaders plays three notes on a recorder (or on a flute, or strikes a bell three times), calling the participants in. All the participants are ritually smudged and psychically cleansed, with a burning sage stick. The leader(s) stand at the gateway to welcome the participants.[1]

Each one entering receives an embrace, a ritual kiss of welcome, and a greeting. It is customary for these greetings to be done cross-gender, with the female leader greeting the males and vice-versa. Each participant and the greeter say to each other, "Merry meet."

Each participant enters the circle in turn, in alternating sequence according to the gender of their spirit. Each walks in a *sun-*

---

[1] In all our earlier work we wrote of *flamen* and *flamenca*, the old Latin Keepers of the Sacred Flame; but that usage has not resonated with the alternative community. Here we use *leaders* as a nongender-specific, inclusive, generic, baggage-free term. The leader(s) may be singular or plural, and of any gender and sexual orientation.

wise[2] direction to their place around the perimeter so that all are evenly spaced, still in alternate psychic gender order. As each enters, (s)he embraces each one already in the circle.

When everyone is in, usually the female leader closes the outermost circle with a line of sulfur while the male leader throws a little sulfur on the central fire.[3]

Leader: "Spirits and forces of evil, you may not cross this line. Spirits and forces of good, come to us. All spirits and forces above and below, hear now my warning. If any be evil or malicious, you will be trapped in this circle if you do not leave now. Leave and hold your peace."

All: "Evil spirits and forces above us, below us, and around us: Go now or forever hold your peace."

Male Leader: "Evil spirits and forces, see how sulfur burns."

Leader (closing the circle gate with a line of sulfur): "If you cross this line, the sulfur will surely burn you. Spirit guides and friends, we will not harm you. Come in joy and peace."

The participants raise their athames.

All: "See, oh spirits and forces of evil, how sharp and holy are our athames."

If the circle is meeting outdoors, the athames are stabbed into the soil between the outer two circles and remain vertical with the sharpened edge facing outward away from the center of the circle. If the meeting is indoors, athames are laid flat (again with the sharpened edge outward) and their points to the left as participants face outward.

Leader: "Let these herbs of the earth remind us of our intent. We seal this circle with earth."

---

[2]In the northern hemisphere, sunwise is clockwise or *deosil*. In the southern hemisphere, it is counterclockwise or *widdershins*.
[3]This and subsequent actions can be done by either leader. Gender is of little or no importance in most of the steps.

Between the two outer circles the participants use the herb the leader gives them to strew a continuous line around the circle.

All: "Let the energies from these herbs aid us in our work this night, and seal this our circle. As we will, so let it be." All look downward. "Gaea, we honor you and thank you for your bounty."

Leaders move to the altar or fireplace at the center. They light four candles: one each of green, red, blue, and white. Each leader picks up two candles. Holding the candles high before them, they walk completely around the inside of the circle.

Leaders: "I seal this circle with fire."

All: "We seal this circle with fire. As we will, so let it be."

When the leaders arrive at the easternmost point inside the circle, all participants turn to face east. They make the moon sign with their hands.

Moon Sign

All (including Leaders): "Spirits of the east, see this guiding light. Come with the rising sun and moon to visit us. Here at the east we honor all newborns and new beginnings. As we will, so let it be."[4]

The female leader places a green candle just inside the closed circle. The leaders move to the south, and all turn to face south. They make a fire sign with their hands.

Fire Sign

---

[4]The elements and directions we use here are inspired by European tradition. If you live on the Atlantic coast of the United States, water should probably be in the east and air in the west. If you live in the southern hemisphere, fire should probably be in the north and water or ice in the south (as being closer to Antarctica). Do not slavishly follow the element directions if they do not fit your geographic location.

All: "Spirits to the south, see this guiding light. Come from the heat of the noonday sun to be with us, bringing your inspiration, warmth, and energy to our ritual. We honor you and the fire of inspiration and the energy of youth. As we will, so let it be."

A red candle is placed close to the outermost circle at the south point. The leaders move to the westernmost point. All turn to face west. They make an earth sign with their hands.

Earth Sign

All: "Spirits of the west, see this guiding light. Come from the earth and visit us. We honor the gifts you bring of craftsmanship and harvest. As we will, so let it be."

A blue candle is placed close to the outer circle. The leaders move to the north. All turn to face north. They make a water sign with their hands.

Water Sign

All: "Spirits to the north, see this guiding light. Come from the cold to visit us. We honor the wisdom of age that you bring to help us in our work. As we will, so let it be."

Leader places a white candle close to the outermost circle in the north.

The leaders move to the altar and pour some water into four non-magnetic bowls. They walk around the circle, sprinkling water from the top bowl. They affirm, "With the water which all living things need, we seal this circle."

All: "As we will, so let it be."

The leaders place a water bowl near each candle. They return to the altar and pick up the remaining candle, the sage smudging-stick, and the fan. They move around the circle wafting smoke.

All: "We seal this circle with the breath of life." All look up. "Spirits above,[5] we invite you and honor you for the air we breathe and for the gentle rain of life. As we will, so let it be."

The leaders move to the altar and take up a non-magnetic bowl of friable earth or sand. They walk around the circle, sprinkling the earth from the bowl while they affirm, "Mother, with Your body we seal this circle." The circle will now look as shown in Figure X-1.

Now that the outer circle is closed and sealed with earth, fire, water, and air, it is appropriate to raise energy. Normally you will start with a dance to music that alternates a fast rhythm with a slow. Depending on the number of participants and on the size of the circle, you can use either a simple grapevine step (ask any trained dancer) or what we call The Shuffle (left foot to the left, close right foot to it, left foot again to the left). As each fast section of music ends, the male role-players turn to their right and move one partner to their right. All too soon this piece is over and the fast step repeats. The music will tell you which pattern to perform. Four or five repetitions of this sequence are usually enough to get everyone ready to send out the energy.

An important piece of ritual now occurs: the god-bargain. It takes two forms. Either a valued object is broken or burned in the fire, or the male role-players lie on their backs and the female role-players mount them so that introitus can occur. The female role-players lift their arms and say,

"Spirit witnesses, see now that we give up our pleasure for the sake of _____ (the intent of the ritual)."

All stand and briefly join hands. Then they break the hold and place their palms with fingers parallel to those of the person next to them, with all thumbs pointing to the left, with palms separated by about 1 inch. The energy starts to flow around this circle. As a chant

---

[5]Many groups use the Native American phrase "Grandfather Sky."

begins and builds, the energy will grow until it is a living, moving entity. At the height of the chant, all yell the intent.

The normal chant in our circles is a repetition of the syllables "Aye-oh" starting softly and gently, and building louder and faster to a climax. Workers breathe at will during the chant. At the climax, all scream out the intent and the leaders clap out the altar candle. For your specific intent, look up the chant in Appendix One, Table 4. If your wish list contains more than one item, you may retrieve some of the power by dancing and chanting a second time. This will give another (though lower) peak.

When the work is complete,

Leaders: "Let any remaining energy go into the water."

All: "As we will, so let it be."

The leader opens the circle: "I open now the gate to our temple. Spirits and guides, protect this circle until we return."

Everyone leaves and goes to prearranged bowers to get grounded and adjust their endorphins. In about thirty minutes, a leader plays three notes on a recorder to recall the participants. The leader opens the circle and re-welcomes them. Participants may bring chairs in with them (see below). When everyone is inside, the leader closes all three circles with sulfur and the original affirmations.

Participants all face outward and use salt to draw the astrological symbols between the two innermost circles. Figure X-1 shows how the circle looks now.

The leaders pick up a basket of bread from the altar.

Leaders: "Gaea and Wheat Spirits, we thank you for your gift."
The bread is passed around the circle; each participant feeds the next one in line with a little of the bread and says, "Honor the gift of bread. May the spirit within you flourish."

The leaders return to the altar and bless the chalice of wine.

Leaders: "Gaea and the Spirit of the Grape, we honor you and thank you for your gift."

Each participant takes a good drink of wine and presents the chalice to the next in line, saying, "Thou art god" to the males and

"Thou art goddess" to the females. The wine aides in relaxation and in attaining homeostasis. (Those who elect not to ingest alcohol may use grape juice.)

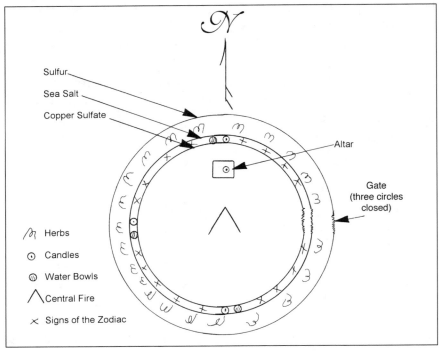

Figure X-1
Ritual Circle with Three Gates Closed

Everyone sits, either on the non-magnetic chairs that they brought in after the interlude, or comfortably cross-legged. Most prefer to face east. If there is room for participants to lie down, they lie with heads to the north. The leader uses a guided meditation similar to that in Chapter Two; or if the participants are skilled, they can meditate on their own.

During this time both leaders stay alert and awake to stand guard over the bodies of those who do meditate or travel. It is their task to make sure that everyone is protected, both physically and psychically.

The circle is taken down in the reverse order that it was constructed. At the north quarter, the leaders lift the candle and blow it out.

All: "Spirits and friends, we thank you for your presence here tonight. Go now to your lovely realms, harming none on the way. Merry meet, and merry part, and merry meet again. As we will, so let it be."

The same is repeated at west, south, east, the sky, and the earth. The leader opens all three gates, steps outside the circle, and says goodbye to each participant with a repetition of the words "Merry meet, merry part, and merry meet again." The circles are carefully brushed away and the materials collected to be scattered or buried, ideally at a crossroads.

The whole group should now have a meal. After the meal you should discuss and analyze your experience. Analysis should examine both whether the *intent* was correct and whether your *technique* was the best one for that specific intent. Pay special attention to the results from the meditation period, both as regards the ritual and for any guidance that individual participants received. Now it is time to disperse, regretfully, to your respective homes. Remember that in the following weeks you must continue to analyze and expect results—both in the target and in the participants. Always remember that there may be transformations either in one or several parties.

"Not Applicable" Is Not an Answer

You can adapt the master ritual. It is always applicable to any situation. Yes, it may seem difficult or complicated; it may seem overly detailed and a lot of work. But just how badly do you want that dream to come true? It works—and, as the advertisers say, if it works, don't fix it.

We have used this master ritual format for more than thirty years. It came to us from a coven group in Cornwall in southwest England, via the coven that initiated Gavin almost fifty years ago. How long they had been using it (successfully), and how long the people *they* got it from had been using it, we have no way of knowing; but we suspect that it came from the mid-1800s. Thus we can say with confidence that the master ritual format is well over a hundred years old. Elements of the same ritual format show up in other occult paths and ceremonies, though not necessarily in the most effective sequence. And some of those rituals, such as Masonic temple initiations, are also very old. Thus the format is validated and authenticated by age and longevity.[6] In addition thousands upon thousands of our students have found it effective—so modern usage as well validates it. We say again, whether you work alone or with a group, it is always applicable. You don't need to reinvent the wheel.

---

[6] If it weren't effective, surely it would not have survived so long.

Chapter Eleven

What Happened?

Something Did Too Happen

An essential part of any ritual is the follow-up, the figuring-out of what happened, either to the participants or to the target. A follow-up analysis of events may be even more important in the early months of your ritual work than it will be when you get your system grooved in. Once that happens, you will be more confident and better skilled at tuning yourself and others to the intent. Occasionally unusual results—surprising results—happen. Identifying the *how* and the *why* of such results will lead you to better-constructed rituals.

When you work to direct and to release energy, something always happens. That something may not be immediately evident, but with careful checking and follow-up you will learn a great deal.

When you do your ritual, you change the fabric of the space/time continuum. Somewhere something will happen. Ideally, that something will be the fulfillment of your ritual's intent. The results may not be readily apparent. Have patience. Eventually they will become apparent: The thing you worked for will manifest itself.

BRAD'S FATHER WINS THE LOTTERY

Brad L's father Calvin lived in Des Moines, Iowa. Retired and on a fixed income, he was always lamenting to Brad that he never had the money to do anything he wanted. Brad himself was one of those relaxed individuals who takes life as it comes. He had never been a great success—nor yet a failure—so he lived alone, still playing the field comfortably but without any real spare cash to help Cal. Brad was an inveterate player of the lottery. Ten years ago he had given up smoking, and he decided he would put the cigarette money into lottery tickets. He had his favorite lucky numbers, and they had won him some small amounts over the years—no really big money, but enough to keep him interested—to tease him along.

Cal got interested in Brad's winnings and suggested that he would like to bet with Brad. Brad did not object, since it was more amusement than serious gambling. From the moment Cal got involved, Brad won nothing. In fact his numbers weren't even close to the winning ones. Brad gradually lost interest, but Cal kept on playing. When Brad began to investigate the occult, he wondered whether he could use his newly acquired pendulum talents to choose himself some new lottery numbers. Of course he told Cal about them, and Cal started betting on them. Those new numbers too won him nothing. Brad stopped betting, but got Cal another set of numbers and almost immediately Cal began to win—not the million dollars everyone hopes for, but at least several hundreds.

THE LAW OF SILENCE

In recounting all this to us, Brad wondered why Cal's kiss of death had changed to winning. We told him that it's very unusual for anyone to win on numbers they share with others. There seems to be a law of silence, and sharing magical results dramatically reduces its effectiveness. This does not apply to sharing the results *after* the effect has manifested; in fact, sharing the positive results may often spur a group on to do more. We told Brad that if Cal was genuinely hard up and he, Brad, was emotionally involved in having Cal win, then he might try getting a number for Cal and not sharing it.

Brad decided that in fact it was more a game with Cal than an urgent necessity; so he tried our suggestion first with Sonia, a woman friend at work, who was genuinely broke. Sure enough, a win resulted. Sonia was thrilled beyond words when she got a win in the thousands of dollars. A side effect of this little ritual was that Sonia, Brad, and her five-year-old daughter began living together. They are now happily handfasted.[1]

The ritual intent was: *Solve Sonia's money problems!* Brad is more than happy with the results, and their family is expanding. They now have two more children and another on the way. If it hadn't worked out positively, Brad would have had only himself to blame. The intent was too wide and open to many results. An intent like: *winning lottery number for Sonia* would have limited the possible outcomes.

Errors in Ritual Lead to Strange Results

The most common error in ritual is in defining the intent. Intent has to be defined in the minds of all participants as *clearly* as possible, and the words of the affirmation must be short and telegraphic. Without care, these two requirements become mutually exclusive. We have told the tale many times of the ladies of our coven doing a ritual for more men. The result was that soon a very charming group of gay men applied for membership. That was not quite what the ladies had intended. You must think your intent through. Do not leave blanks on your order form; instead, narrow down the random choices that force the magic to guess your intent.

A very common error occurs in the wording. The distinction may be subtle, but outcomes can be disastrous. Think about the affirmation "I *want* money." If you do a ritual with that as your intent, you will continually *want* money. Instead, the affirmation

---

[1]Handfasting: a spiritual rite of passage implying much the same as marriage.

might be "Money, money, come to me" or something similar. Relationship rituals, too, often run into trouble. They are, after all, caging rituals. Consequently, when you really do get that blond bombshell into your life—and discover you have only a bed in common—you can't get rid of him or her. And there is no real way of doing a ritual that says "I'd like to get the blond bombshell out of my life." In general such things occur because you were lax in your definition.

Non-return rituals and caging rituals are always dangerous. What we mean by this is: If you put all your effort into caging that wonderful Significant Other—then realize it's been a mistake—it can be extremely difficult to end the relationship. A clever friend of ours posited, "What do you do? Take him to the used-lover dealer?"

Mistakes will occur, so be very careful of the non-reversible ritual. If, at the height of a ritual, you burn the piece of paper on which you wrote the intent, or burn a candle impressed with the intent, you can't unburn them. On the other hand, if you make a true lover's knot that combines your hair with the hair of your target, it can be undone.[2]

In doing healing rituals, the most common thing that happens is that the patient is cured of the disease for which the ritual was designed, but they promptly get some other disease—usually more life-threatening than the cured one. This happens because the ritual did not cure the *underlying* discontent or stress that made the first disease necessary to the patient. That disease at which you aim your ritual is only the outward symptom of some deeper dysfunction. The patient *needs* the disease—for whatever reason, whether it be just for getting attention, or because they don't want that promotion for which they don't feel fitted, or whatever.

The ritual did not fail. It cured the disease and it didn't *cause* the replacement illness. The patient caused the new disease. When you follow up, then, be quite specific. Did the ritual cure the disease it was aimed at? This means, of course, that the intent had to be specific. Just *"Heal Aunt Agnes!"* doesn't do it. Instead it had to specify

---

[2]A video of "Love Spells" is available from Godolphin House, P.O. Box 297-B, Hinton, WV 25951, and at www.wicca.org.

a disease. In your follow-up analysis, investigate these ideas: What purpose did the disease serve? Why does the patient need an illness? What is it buying him?

The Timing of the Results

Magical results cannot contravene the basic laws of physics. If, for instance, it were possible suddenly to manifest a baseball, then that manifestation would cause something akin to an atomic explosion. Magic has to work slowly. The one exception to that cardinal rule is in changes of mental state, whether of the target or of the practitioner. Mental states can be changed instantly. Thus when you think of results, you can look for immediate changes in attitude; but in every other aspect, you need to keep a little diary for at least a month after the ritual. Some occultists view this as changing the future and allowing that future change to come down the River of Time to you. Discipline and patience are therefore of prime importance when you look for the results of ritual. Don't expect the money to manifest in your wallet the day you do the ritual. Instead, look for longer-term results. Do not expect the cancerous tumor to disappear instantly. It will go in its own good time.

Occasionally results are very rapid, though they have still taken an appreciable amount of time on the cosmic scale. Yvonne did a healing on a lady reporter one day, and the next day the woman was found to be free of the leukemia that she had thought would shortly kill her. In this case, interestingly enough, it was another unexpected result. Yvonne was working to heal a migraine headache. She had not known of the leukemia at all. Yvonne quite inadvertently healed the leukemia as well as the headache. Her intent was obviously too wide. In this case as in Brad's, though, the results were positive.

Knowing that things are unpredictable, that results take time, in your Book of Light you will want to keep accurate records of the original intent, exactly what affirmation, mind keys, and psychic links you used, the timing information, and the long-term results. We usually check results for some three months after the date of any ritual. Although there is no actual time limit on the results, three months seems a reasonable span of time to us.

In certain rare cases the target may be learning a karmic lesson. Whatever the problem is, it may not go away before the lesson is adequately learned. The only way to determine this is through meditation and contact with the patient's Guides. Many people contact their own Guide and channel quite adequately that way; they forget that you can also channel to somebody else's Guides.

Analysis and Desire versus Reality

It is a bitter pill for some people to take, that the magic does sometimes fit itself to your real world. You have fallen in love with that wondrous unattainable person, perhaps one who is a film star (or you think should be) and your ritual result brings you into contact with someone who does not exactly match your fantasy intent. Perhaps it would be as well for you to step back and realize that at your income level the fantasy figure would be impossible to keep. Even if you managed a first date, it would become clear very quickly that this person is not for you. In a similar way, a lust for a ton of gold or all the money in the world is often going to be fulfilled, but by a more moderate amount. In analyzing your results, you should always take this into account.

Reality has an unwelcome way of intruding into the results of many rituals. Plain Bill or Jim may be just the person you need in your life, so don't reject them out of hand on the assumption that they don't fulfill your fantasy.

Why and How Did Lavinia Get Her New Car?

Lavinia E lived in Tampa, Florida. Anyone who has seen Tampa knows that the traffic proceeds apace along some of those grand boulevards. Lavinia's old car just couldn't seem to keep up. It was continually breaking down. She worked at the same place as the lady whose story we told before, whose boss gave her a Cadillac. Lavinia was determined to get herself a new car magically.

Since it was going to be a magic car, she decided that it had to be a Lamborghini in fire-engine red. Why not go for broke? With a price tag of over $100,000, very few Lamborghinis are imported into the United States. Not daunted by that fact, Lavinia gathered a small group of friends and did a ritual for her Lamborghini. The very next evening she was in a terrible accident. A drunk driver ran a red light and broadsided her old rust-bucket, landing her in the intensive-care unit. She stayed in intensive care several days before she was moved off the critical list, but it was nearly a month before she got out of the hospital. The man who had hit her had tested for a blood alcohol level of over 0.2. Wanting to settle, the insurance company offered Lavinia $250,000—a quarter-million dollars.

They finally settled for a little over $300,000. She could probably have gotten more if she'd been strong enough to go through a long court battle.

She put most of the money into a good reliable mutual bond fund. With the rest she bought a brand-new Honda 2000 convertible in fire-engine red. This was when they were first on the market, and she paid the dealer's full asking price, including the iniquitous four-thousand-dollar "preparation" fee. Believe it or not, she still wanted her magic Lamborghini. Somehow money to buy a car wasn't the same thing as getting a real automobile.

Hospital bills had taken a fair chunk of her settlement and she was not willing to spend most of the remaining money on the Lamborghini. She still insisted that she would magic it. Despite the advice of all her friends, she did another ritual for her fantasy dream car. This time—probably fortunately—nothing at all happened. She was about to do a third ritual when a friend had a brainwave. At a model store she bought a small plastic red Lamborghini replica. Surreptitiously she put it on Lavinia's coffee table.

It totally satisfied Lavinia. She had her Lamborghini.

Of course her friends teased her that she had screwed up the ritual by failing to stipulate a "real" Lamborghini, and that was why she had gotten the replica. Obviously the forces that guide our fates had decided that a Honda convertible was more in keeping with Lavinia's lifestyle and had provided it for her, though at quite a painful price.

No amount of further rituals for the Lamborghini would have been successful.

This little story makes two points:

1. Reality once again interposed itself in the ritual results.
2. Lavinia had not been specific enough in the definition of the Lamborghini she wanted. It doesn't really matter that her friend, the instrument of fate, went out and bought her one. She got her Lamborghini.

THE LINE OF LEAST RESISTANCE

Imagine water running out onto the ground. If there is any slope at all, it will run downhill along its path of least resistance. We have come to believe that magic is like water. It takes the path that uses the least energy. That path may look circuitous, even devious; but the water has no trouble flowing.

Sometimes the factors in your life may be so at variance with your ritual intent that the answer *looks like* "No"—yet something always happens. In considering what might go wrong, look at the ritual from the point of view of what would be the easiest solution, remembering that magic may not have the same world view that you have. In Lavinia's case, a bad accident that landed her in the hospital got her the insurance money to buy a new car.

Is that the sort of thing that might happen to you? If you did a ritual for increased sexual activity, might it not be that the hard-up unattractive person in your work place would suddenly arrive in your bed? When you try to cure Grandma's cancer, the line of least resistance—and maybe the best solution for Grandma too—might well be that she should "die." That's not the stereotypical happy ending, but it is a logical one.

In today's world we do try to keep people alive far longer than is wise or helpful for their spiritual development. We believe that once a person enters a persistent vegetative state with no hope of recovery, spending thousands of dollars on postponing the inevitable is negative on two counts:

1. (Perhaps the more important) What is the patient *learning* by being kept alive in a vegetative state?
2. What proportion of the planet's resources is being invested in prolonging the mere presence of vital signs in the patient? Might not those resources be better invested elsewhere?

Was the Trade-off Worth It?

Was Lavinia's new car worth the accident? Although she recovered after a long time in intensive care, full mobility will return to her body only after some years—if it ever does. She's driving a bright new sports car and is content. If you ask her, she will tell you it was worth it.

When you go for that new management position and the ritual lands it for you, are the extra work and stress and the consequent deterioration of your health worth the few extra bucks you'll garner from the change? What about the power lunches? Are they reward enough for the tense stomach and the nights you sleep with one foot on the floor?

So your new love ritual worked? The old Significant Other is out of your life? The cost in upheaval, dollars, and heartache may seem worth it while the honeymoon glow is still with you; the sex is much better. Having a younger person on your arm when you dine out garners you many envious glances. You feel more alive. But it's costing you a bundle—and maybe if you had spent more time talking and working with the old discarded Significant Other, that relationship could have been renewed and the trauma avoided. Your shared history might not have been lost.

Relationships take serious work. Too many people see the greener grass and think the new relationship won't have the problems of the old. Be assured it will, if you are not willing to spend the time to make it work.

Americans lament to each other that we have a Kleenex® society—throw away the old one and get a new one. Use it; throw it away. People are not Kleenexes®, though we tend to treat them as if they were.

Real Results or Coincidence?

It's no good just doing a ritual for companionship until you put yourself in the way of meeting new people. We recommend taking a course in a subject that interests you—going dancing—getting a new hobby—all things that lead to introductions to many new friends. When did you last do volunteer work for a non-profit organization? Pick work or play in which you are interested, then the new friends will have interests in common with your interests. Whatever you do, don't pick a hobby such as jogging or home exercise or stamp collecting. Each of those is a lonely—a solitary—pursuit. You need to choose something that will put you in personal contact with many new faces.

So you do a ritual for a new companion and at the same time you increase your contact list—and suddenly there (s)he is! Is it a coincidence, or is it the result of the ritual? Would it have happened without the ritual? Who knows? We think it is unlikely, especially if, without reading this advice, you had just carried on in your old patterns.

What if you just decided to meet new people without the benefit of any preliminary ritual work? Does that constitute magic? If you have changed yourself as you take the new track, the answer may well be "Yes." And thus in some way, at some level, you *have* used magic. How can you tell whether that person would have come into your life anyway? You could try channeling; but it's unlikely that you'll ever know what really made it happen.

In any event, be grateful. Don't look that proverbial gift horse in the mouth. A friend of ours, Joe L, lives in Chicago, Illinois. He told us, he had barely completed his ritual when he heard a knock at the door. His new next-door neighbor wanted to use his phone; hers had not yet been connected. She was immediately interested in the ritual equipment that still stood in his living room, and asked a tactful question; the rest is history. They are living together with plans for a handfasting next year.

That's a pretty rare occurrence; don't count on the same thing happening to you. There's a saying:

The gods help those who help themselves.

CHANGE TAKES TIME

As we have said, change takes time. Things don't happen in a flash or with a snap of your fingers. Work Sheet XI-1 is designed to remind you over a longer period of time that you did something and that events are working toward the fulfillment of your need. The left-hand column lists some standard basic needs, with blank spaces where you can enter unlisted things that are important to you. In the blank column headed Ritual Date, you will enter a date against whichever intent you worked for. Then in the three columns for results you can note any consequences that may have happened in one week, one month, and three months.

Intent	Ritual Date	One Week	One Month	Three Months
Protection				
Healing				
Companion				
Wealth				
Other				

Work Sheet XI-1
Effects of Rituals

Keep this chart up to date. Note the results. We reiterate that things *will* happen. If you do not stay alert for them, you may inadvertently miss some significant change that comes into your life.

Don't Just Walk Away

All too often people run a ritual; then when there are no immediate vivid results, they write it off as a failure and forget about it. We encourage you here not just to walk away from a ritual into which you have put a lot of effort because (as we keep saying) *something* has happened somewhere in the cosmos. Those happenings may not immediately be apparent. Manifesting takes time. And they come about in surprising ways. Be confident that you knew what you were doing and that you will get results. Thousands upon thousands of people—who are probably less intelligent than you, and who have not had the benefit of the training that this book offers—have performed successful, effective rituals.

Be confident that something has happened. It's up to you to recognize exactly what that something was. Be alert. Trust us. We've been doing this probably since before you were born. It always works. Don't doubt that something has happened. But do question whether you have overlooked something in the intent or in the results, and consequently the result is not exactly as you hoped it would be. If you persistently invest energy in the idea that it hasn't worked and isn't going to, then you're putting out a lot of negative energy that may actually neutralize the positive ritual results that you worked for and expect. When a child has a sore or an injury, we tell her not to pick at it. Let it heal. We tell you exactly the same thing for a ritual:

Don't pick at it.

Let it run its course, even if that course takes longer than you want.

There's a twenty-first-century pattern—the instant-gratification syndrome—that Magic hasn't yet caught on to. Magic doesn't seem to be in the instant-gratification business. It is not into the modern wonder-drug, miracle-working, whiz-bang, blue-balls-of-fire thing. For reasons we don't always comprehend, it takes its own sweet time to work. It doesn't manifest overnight any more than a beautiful garden would. Yes, occasionally when needs be and someone is in dire need of healing it happens quickly. But most other needs, such as money, a new job, or a new companion, aren't that urgent. If it's going to happen, it will happen. Let it be.

TODAY'S ERRORS, TOMORROW'S SUCCESSES

We all let our desires outrun our objectivity. Working to have a film-star in your life probably won't succeed. And when your ritual does come true, you may regret it and realize that it was an error. If you do a *non-return* ritual with a poorly defined intent and get an erroneous and surprising result, imagine now how difficult it is to fix that.

A careful and thorough study of the results of any ritual, together with an analysis of the original intent as you defined it, will equip you to make sure that future rituals are more on target and even more effective.

CHAPTER TWELVE

YOUR RITUAL LIFE

Many people find life bland and uninteresting. Day follows day, you work hard, you spend your money, the debts never seem to go away, the pressures don't let up, and the little frustrations of life are ever-present. Once you embark on the magical ritual path, life will never be dull or boring again.

WHERE ARE YOU IN YOUR LIFE?

The life of people in western society proceeds through several distinct stages. The Ancients realized centuries ago that each phase lasted something like seven years, and that fact holds true today. At 7 years old, you are in the early stages of your formal education. At 14 years you are a teenager. At 21 you reach legal majority. At 28 many people get their first divorce. At 35 career change is in the air. Forty-two is a major decision point: Either you strike out in new directions or you resign yourself to the current situation. Each seven-year cycle is a subset of a longer twenty-eight year cycle that in the occult world is called a *Saturn cycle* because a "year" on Saturn—one revolution about the sun—takes twenty-eight-plus Earth years.

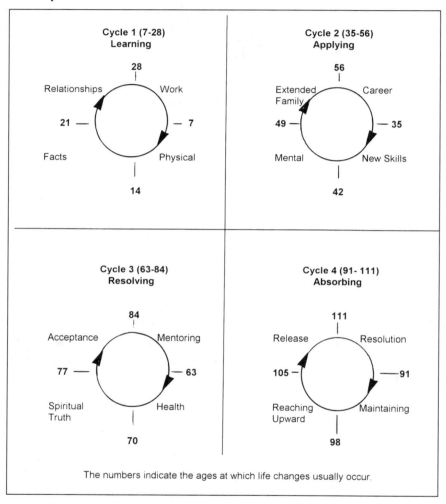

Figure XII-1
The Saturn Cycle

Figure XII-1 shows a sequence of four typical Saturn cycles, the great development plan in a typical human life. In the Spiral of Life each turn around the circle moves you to a higher level of your spirit's basic learning. The names we have given each seven-year segment are our suggestions; you can use similar names if you like them better. Use your chronological age to get you close to where you should be in the Saturn cycles, then decide whether you are lagging or ahead of your life learning curve. Do you have time left to finish the segment? Should you have moved on long ago? Do the intents of your planned rituals move you forward on your own great spiral of life?

Whatever phase you are in, it is good to concentrate on working at and completing that aspect of your learning. Realize that where you are is where you are supposed to be; that things are really all right. There is no need to chafe restlessly and long for something different. Instead of denying the work that is appropriate to this stage, use your rituals to get the most out of the experiences in which you find yourself and to help you move through smoothly to the next phase.

The most important aspect of this spiral? Don't get stuck in one of its segments. Let's imagine you are between 21 and 28, exploring relationships. How many people do you know who are still exploring when they should have committed and moved on? Similarly, how many workaholics do you know? Those people too should move on.

In Wiccan/pagan groups the four levels are sometimes named differently. Table XII-1 lists some typical choices.

Learning	Maiden	Youth
Applying	Mother	Father
Resolving	Elder	Elder
Absorbing	Crone	Sage

Table XII-1
Alternative Names for Segments of the Saturn Spiral

Making Your Habits Work for You

As we see it, rituals can help you in many ways.

1. *Life-maintenance* rituals are those simple things such as brushing your teeth, getting your possessions together for the next day at the office or at the beach, perhaps preparing meals. The more

you get these life-maintenance tasks organized and routine, the easier they can become. Women especially face the challenge of selecting and wearing a different outfit to the office every day. If you put together five or six complete sets of appropriate clothing, you can pull just one hanger from the wardrobe and be sure that everything you need for that day is there.

Ritualizing your meals is another way to make life easier. Remember the time when fish-on-Fridays was simply a given, with no thought required? Plan a week's menus ahead, buy all the food on one trip, and you will ease that never-ending part of your life. Don't be afraid of planning ahead.

2. The *mundane* rituals that we discuss throughout this book are designed to bring that extra magical pressure to bear, to manifest in your life the things you need. This book will aid you in planning those rituals ahead, but you will also need a calendar lest the sheer number of rituals overwhelm you. Your work in Chapter Seven showed you that certain rituals must occur on definite dates but that others can move a day or two. Korean shamans do their major magical rituals three days later than western Witches do. They say there is a delay in the gravitational effects of the sun and the moon; and the tides of the ocean suggest that they are at least partially right. So you can confidently postpone certain of your rituals by a day or two to bring them into a more convenient time slot.

June		July	
2–3	Weekend	5	Full Moon–Thur
5	Full Moon–Tue	7–8	Weekend
9–10	Weekend	14–15	Weekend
16–17	Weekend	20	New Moon–Fri
21	New Moon and Solstice–Thur	21–22	Weekend
23–24	Weekend	28–29	Weekend
30–1	Weekend		

Table XII-2 — Interlocking Cycles of Life and Ritual (2001)

Look at the calendar of June and July 2001 in Table XII-2. The ritual for full moon of June 5 occurs on a Tuesday; postponement to the weekend would rob it of its effectiveness. Nor can a ritual for new moon and solstice, June 21, be moved, because solstice is a fixed astronomical event. Yet in July both full and new moons could feasibly move to the subsequent weekend.

In planning mundane rituals, consider the interplay between the "real" world and the ritual world so that the two can interface smoothly.

3. A third type of ritual that many of us do is those rituals designed to be *spiritually uplifting*. Many of us add solstice and equinox rituals to our calendar. These are normally not very serious or what might be called heavy rituals; instead they are of a reenergizing, uplifting type. In them we acknowledge and honor our debt of gratitude to Gaea and to the planet on which we live.

Amanda and Ted Remarry

Amanda and Ted R live in Birmingham, Alabama. Both grew up in fundamentalist Baptist families and went to a Baptist church school. They were sweethearts throughout high school. At graduation they wanted to marry immediately, but their families persuaded them to wait a little while. They finally married when both were twenty, knowing very little about Life—or about sex. The bedroom was a sad disappointment to Ted, and a place that Amanda did not particularly like. Pretty soon Ted developed a roaming eye. Some seven years later they divorced and Ted moved out to investigate the singles scene.

He began exploring the occult. In parallel, he attended the Baptist church's singles meetings, and often saw Amanda there. He told her of his new interest, and was surprised when she expressed interest too. Although there was still some bitterness in both of them over the breakup, they agreed that their marriage hadn't been all that bad and maybe they should study this new field together. They attended several regularly scheduled classes. The more they learned, the more interested they became. Amanda was especially drawn to the ecological and feminist aspects of the Craft, and Ted felt attracted to magic. Their new growth alienated them from the Baptist church and from Amanda's parents; Ted's family was more accepting of their branching out. Ted and Amanda agreed their duty to their own spirits was greater than that to their church.

The class moved into Tantra and the raising of kundalini through gender differences. Amanda was not ready to take other partners, so she and Ted agreed to practice together. Their practice led them to resume living together. With their new interest and the ever-changing ritual year, the boredom and ennui that had plagued their earlier life together disappeared, especially since Ted's singles experiences had much improved his skills as a lover. This encouraged Amanda to talk to several women of the group about sex. Pretty soon with Ted she had one of those earth-shattering bells-and-whistles first orgasms.

They continued to live together, seeing no reason to remarry until Amanda became pregnant. Everyone in the group was so enthusiastic about the pregnancy, and Amanda and Ted were so overjoyed by it that, for the sake of the child, they decided to remarry. The marriage has endured. They now have three children, and for them all life is an ever-changing kaleidoscope of serenity and gratitude.

Single versus Group

As you progress in ritual, you may want to join a group. Perhaps you have a Significant Other and both of you are interested in ritual; you will still find that group work is rewarding. Your interaction with the group in ritual and the need to work for the goals of other people will teach you a great deal about the raising and sending-out of power for specific intents. We encourage you to attend a couple of large Wiccan/pagan gatherings to get a feel for the kaleidoscope of practices, beliefs, mindsets, and sets of assumptions in that world before you decide to join any group. In other words, shop around.

You will find various groups that offer teaching. Not all may be totally positive. Like members of any group, religious or secular, Witches and pagans endure a certain number of fools and charlatans among their number. There are some leaders who seem to believe they have the right to have sex with anyone who joins the group.

That is not what it's about.

Many clues can signal a poor group and poor leaders. Such fools and charlatans can get you into very negative situations—even into legal problems.

ATTITUDE	WHAT THE LEADERS SAY/DO	YOUR COMFORT LEVEL
1. Sex		
2. Dogmatism		
3. Rigidity		
4. Answering Questions		
5. Attire		
6. Prohibitions		
7. Legality		
8. Awareness		
9. Beliefs		
10. Other		

Work Sheet XII-1
Group Evaluation Work Sheet

Work Sheet XII-1 will help you evaluate any candidate group. The left column, Attitude, lists a number of variables you will want to consider. The next two columns are for you to complete. The one titled "What the Leaders Say/Do" is intended to alert you that what they *profess* may not always harmonize perfectly with what they *do*—whether the discrepancy is conscious or unconscious. The degree of separation between claims and actuality may be quite difficult to ascertain until you talk at length with several members of the group: Do the leaders speak truth or not?

Let's look at each item of the Attitude column in turn.

1. Sex. Are the leaders going to interfere with your sex life? All choices about your sex life should be entirely your own—not subject to the influence or control of a group leader.

2. Dogmatism. Do they make assertions such as "It's true because I say it's true" or "I'm the final authority on that"? A Witch's path is one of learning and understanding. The leaders should be able to help you learn and understand a truth, not cut you off. If you ask a question, it's because you're ready to learn the answer.

3. Rigidity. Do they claim to have the one and only right and true path? Or are they willing to tolerate and even try other ways? People who profess to have all the Right Answers are dangerous; seek instead those who have Questions.

4. Answering Questions. The two preceding points are joined by this one. If the answer to your very real question is "You're not ready to know that yet," that is simply not acceptable.

5. Attire. Do they insist that you wear certain types of clothing in the outside world? Do they require that long hair be cut off into a prescribed style? Again, these are not acceptable characteristics of a good group.

6. Prohibitions. Do they list books or films that you are not allowed to read or view? Do they have *any* prohibitions? Some prohibitions may be good, for instance: no revealing names of other group members; but most are probably signs of weakness in the leadership.

7. Legality. Are they a legal group? This does not mean: Are they a registered non-profit corporation? It means: Are they a *church* or a *foundation* or a *religious association*? Insist on seeing their paperwork. You can get in deep financial and legal trouble if you associate with a group that has inadequate coverage of any sort. And by the way, how do they deal with underage individuals? The group may have the color of legality about them—may have the jargon right—but may not, in fact, be legal. One way to check their status is to ask whether they can conduct

marriages, funerals, and do other pastoral duties such as visit inmates. Again, listen carefully for any evasive replies. If in doubt read Appendix Two.

8. Awareness. This topic covers a range of ideas. Are they aware of environmental concerns? Are they aware of the planet under their feet, walking respectfully on it? Do they throw their butts and trash on the Mother's face?

9. Beliefs. Are you joining a church with a written alternative spirituality? Or is it just a group trying a few psychic experiments? Worse still, is it a money-making scam? Most important, what is the group's ethical belief set?

10. Other. Quietly form your own subjective opinion of the group. The very first time you walk into someone's home, you may get an immediate feeling of liking or disliking. You may not be able to name a specific factor in the formation of that feeling, but it's there—and you will do well to heed it. Write that feeling into Work Sheet XII-1.

Once you have completed the "What the Leaders Say/Do" column, apply a scale of zero to nine, letting zero mean you have no comfort with what they profess and nine mean that you are very comfortable with what they say. Fill in the "Your Comfort Level" column. This will immediately tell you whether it is a group you will fit into without concerns. If the candidate group earns lots of low scores, that is a sign of at best poor, and at worst what we call "bogus," leadership. Quietly steal away and audition other groups.

İf İt Harm Πone

In the group that we ourselves formed more than thirty years ago, and is still in operation, we use gender differences to drive ritual. We use celibacy to increase the power generated by gender differences. We use food-fasting to cleanse the body and as another deprivation/reward system to drive ritual. We require that members meet sky-clad. We thought then, and we think now, that none of these stipulations harm any participant, including ourselves. Thus we are working within our defined moral and ethical value set. You must decide for yourself whether any or all parts of that system are comfortable for you. The question must always be: Is attaining the intent (the goal) worth at least experimenting with your value set? Do you feel that you can ethically do the activities the group expects as a trade-off for the goal of the ritual?

Your Value Set

You have to decide for yourself where your head is with regard to lust, desire, sex, love, marriage, and long-term commitment. Are you duped by the fashion world, by Hollywood, or by guilt-mongers? Guilt, Shame, and Fear are the Big Three manipulators of human minds.

In our experience, ranging over more than thirty years, we meet many people who have been duped by Western culture and who want that pretty boy or trophy girl as a lover. The people we meet fail to understand that the inner spirit is far more important than outward looks. When we speak in person—a popular workshop is "Opening Up to Love and Intimacy"—we take ten or so couples who *do not know each other* and put them through what we call nonjudgmental listening training. All they do is sit nude in a dimly lit room, holding hands and telling each other about themselves. Every time we do this we find that a couple of people from the group— strangers to each other—form instant attachments. Most of those attachments last. We haven't actually counted how many marriages or long-term relationships have resulted from our encounter groups, but we think there are at least a dozen.

These are people who were strangers before taking that one-hour workshop but told something secret about themselves. They got to know each other's *inner* person, free of clothing and thus free of social image and shields. They liked what they found, and they bonded.

To your mind, our own path might earn many low points in Work Sheet XII-1. Yes, we proudly admit our path is different—

unconventional. Yet at last count it is one that some half-million people have chosen to follow in one variation or another.

Look around you. In today's world domestic violence is still rampant and somewhere, every minute of the day and night, a child is abused. We suggest that one solution to these problems is group living. That does not have to mean a group marriage; it can mean simply a small group of people living more communally and supportively than is possible in a nuclear or a single-parent family. When people talk so glibly about family values, they would do well to consider the single parent trying to make it alone in a very tough world. People are spontaneously forming *intentional* households, in which individuals or couples make a conscious decision: They will live and work jointly for the good of the group and of each member.[1]

Large corporations, churches, and government all hate these arrangements. Corporations hate them because

1. intentional households buy fewer major appliances than nuclear families do; and

2. household members depend less on a steady paycheck than do stand-alone isolated employees.

Churches hate them because groups tend to form their own spiritual alliances *outside* the approved letterheads. Governments hate them because corporations and churches hate them. As a subset of government hate toward intentional households, ironic though it sounds, workers in welfare offices are dependent on welfare "clients"—recipients. Without recipients, social workers would be out of a job. Ergo, they survive according to the number of recipients they process.

Eddie, Randy, Jeanne, and Garnet Break Out

Eddie, Randy, Jeanne, and Garnet were San Francisco hippies, right at the height of the Movement in the late 1960s. Somehow—per-

---

[1] Betty Friedan, *The Fountain of Age* (Simon & Schuster).

haps after coming down from a bad trip—they managed to take a hard look at what they were doing. They decided that their current path led nowhere. Like many of what were later called the Mother Earth News people, they went to the California mountains. In an old abandoned mining town they found enough material to build themselves two houses. Then, halfway through the building project, an epiphany happened. Randy asked, "Why do we need two houses?"

There was a moment of silence; then they all burst out laughing. As they told it, they had a glorious dance and wound up in a universal hug-in.

So they built one house, installed one water pump and one solar-powered generator, and planted one large garden. The children came and were home schooled. Things were tough for several years: fighting for title to their land, having to go on food stamps, and borrowing money from parents and friends. Through this tough learning experience they grew very close. Then came the computer revolution and they learned programming, which they happily did in the fastness of the mountains. All of us were overjoyed when the household earned enough income to wrest clear title to their property from the legal quagmire of the abandoned area.

They still live together, four adults and now five teenagers. Occasionally other people have asked to join the group, but somehow no one has stayed. Others have been unwilling to summon the intestinal fortitude to stick it out with them—once they learned that it implied long hours of hard work with few trips to the mall or the fast-food joint.

Any time you form a small group, the question of income to support it raises its head. A couple of small groups in the United States, as in our example, now write software. Another makes pottery and jewelry. Others do the most varied of self-supporting independent tasks.

The one thing these groups share is their total serenity and happiness. That happiness stems from their security and their autonomy. No big boss is going to downsize them. They have sufficient skills among the group to fix almost anything that goes wrong around the dwelling. There's always someone there to lend a hand

and back them up on the very rare occasions when they get sick. And there's always someone who can look after the children when family members need a respite from each other.

Forming Your Own Group

Sometimes you will need the energy that can only be provided by a dedicated group. If you can't find an existing group, then you should form one of your own. In our very first successful book[2] we went to great lengths to tell people how to form and train a group, and we encourage you to look at these or similar recommendations. Briefly:

1. Rent a post-office box.
2. Place an innocuous ad in a local paper.
3. Meet prospects on neutral ground and find a place away from your house to meet as a group.
4. Start a training program scheduled to last at least six months.
5. Be very definite as to requirements.
   a. No missed classes.
   b. An assigned reading list.
   c. Get pacts signed concerning secrecy and confidentiality.
   d. Payment of dues.

Some people are scared away by the teaching requirements. Members of most new study groups will teach themselves with minimum guidance. Any teaching you do will immensely improve your own grasp of the subject.

Planning Your Future Ritual Life

In Chapter Three we asked you to assess where you are now and where you want to go. Now that we have laid out more options, let's

---

[2]Frost and Frost, *Good Witch's Bible* (Godolphin House).

try it again. Fill in Work Sheet XII-2: Identify the things you need and assign dates to the rituals to get them. If, as we hope, you have at least a working group, then your needs may have to be subordinated to those of the group. Yet without a road map to your future, you may go round in circles or even go backward. You will never succeed in getting to a serene, contented, fulfilling life. Think about emphasizing for yourself serenity, security, and happiness.

My/Our Need	Priority	Date Needed	Ritual Date

Work Sheet XII-2
A Ritual Plan for You and Your Group

Use this chart to work out the best timing. Complete your RAPT Chart. Then go to the mundane calendar and fit the defined rituals into a realistic schedule. Then you can quietly, confidently plan and do the rituals you need.

You can do it. Start now.

Blessed Be.

†ABLES

Disease	Color	Disease	Color
Acne	*Dark Blue*	Hepatitis	Reddish-Yellow
Alcoholism	*Violet*	Impotence	Red
Anemia	*Red*	Jaundice	Yellow/Green
Arthritis	*Dark Red*	Measles	Blue
Asthma	*Dark Orange*	Menstrual Cramps	Orange
Boils	*Greenish-Blue*	Mononucleosis	Orange
Burns	*Turquoise*	Nervousness	Light Orange
Cerebral Palsy	*Lemon*	Phlebitis	Blue
Colds and Flu	*Green*	Polio	Red
Constipation	*Yellow*	Rheumatism	Dark Red
Diabetes	*Dark Yellow*	Varicose Veins	Bluish-Red
Fatigue	*Orange*	Venereal Disease	Green
Headache	Blue		

Table 1
Disease-Color Correspondence

Intent	Planet	Sign	Element	Quality	Color	Stone	Metal	Flower*	Herb	Scent	Symbolic Creature	Body Part	Illness
Courage Exploration Military success Athletic ventures	Mars	Aries	Fire	Cardinal	Scarlet	Ruby	Iron	Geranium	Anemone Radish	Tobacco	Ram	Head	Arthritis Blood pressure Depression Exhaustion
Money Business and commerce	Earth	Taurus	Earth	Fixed	Red	Jade	Nickel	Cowslip	Ground-ivy Carpet bugle	Sandal-wood	Bull	Neck	Polio Melancholy Tuberculosis
Advanced technology Electronics Prediction Writing non-fiction	Lucifer	Gemini	Air	Common/ Mutable	Yellow	Opal	Aluminum	Orchid	Calamint Lavender	Cloves	Magpie	Hands Arms Lungs	Constipation Hepatitis Diabetes
Safe journey Astral travel Writing fiction Gain by water	Moon	Cancer	Water	Cardinal	Amber	Pearl	Silver	Night-scented stock	Poppy Moon-wort	White sandal-wood	Crab	Breast Stomach	Bronchitis Circulation Digestion
Friendship Patronage Create harmony Renew youth	Sun	Leo	Fire	Fixed	Orange	Diamond	Gold	Sunflower	Rosemary Saffron	Saffron	Lion	Heart Spine Arms Wrists	Thyroid Mononucleosis Menstrual cramps
Exams Theater Influence people Merchandise	Mercury	Virgo	Earth	Common/ Mutable	Chart-reuse	Agate	Mercury	Snowdrop	Caraway Bitter-sweet	Cinna-mon	Virgin	Abdomen Hands Intestines	Cerebral palsy Mental retardation Colitis

Table 2

Master Meta–Psychometric Table

*Table 3 shows the botanical names for these flowers and herbs.

Intent	Planet	Sign	Element	Quality	Color	Stone	Metal	Flower	Herb	Scent	Symbolic Creature	Body Part	Illness
Acquire beauty Love, friendship Pleasure Joyous undertakings	Venus	Libra	Air	Cardinal	Emerald	Emerald	Copper	Rose	Alkanet Black-alder	Myrtle	Swan	Lower Back Kidneys	Fever Blood Disease Hypertension
Inheritances Win legal conflict Gratify lust	Pluto	Scorpio	Water	Fixed	Turquoise	Turquoise	Platinum	Cactus	Sweet basil Soapwort	Orange blossom	Scorpion	Pelvis, Genitalia	Boils Burns Impotence Muscle tension
Career Luck and wealth General ambition	Jupiter	Sagittarius	Fire	Common/ Mutable	Blue	Sapphire	Tin	Narcissus	Balm Asparagus	Nutmeg	Centaur	Hips Thighs Liver	Nausea Shingles Goiter
Knowledge of astral Business affairs Study for exams All home matters	Saturn	Capricorn	Earth	Cardinal	Indigo	Onyx	Lead	Thistle	Barley Ivy	Civet	Goat	Knees Bones Skin	Glaucoma Palsy
All unconventional enterprises Esoteric knowledge Disrupt friendship	Uranus	Aquarius	Air	Fixed	Violet	Aqua-marine	Uranium	Buttercup	Winter savory Rhubarb	Lemon	Phoenix	Ankles	Ulcer Epilepsy Diarrhea
Solve mysteries Develop mysticism	Neptune	Pisces	Water	Common	Lavender	Amethyst	Neptun-ium	Water lily	Water betony Thrift	Water lily	Dolphin	Feet	Insomnia Irritation Tumors

Table 2 (Cont'd)
Master Meta–Psychometric Table

Traditional Name	Botanical Name	Traditional Name	Botanical Name	Traditional Name	Botanical Name	Traditional Name	Botanical Name
Alkanet	Anchusa	Cowslip	Caltha	Rose	Rosa		
Anemone	Anemone	Geranium	Pelargonium	Rosemary	Rosmarinus		
Asparagus	Asparagus officinalis	Ground ivy	Nepeta	Saffron	Colchicum		
Balm	Populus candicans, Melissa officinalis, et alii	Ivy	Hedera	Snowdrop	Galanthus		
Barley	Hordeum vulgare	Lavender	Lavandula	Soapwort	Saponaria		
Bittersweet	Celastrus	Moonwort	Menispermum	Sunflower	Helianthus		
Black alder	Alnus	Narcissus	Narcissus	Sweet basil	Ocimum basilicum		
Buttercup	Ranunculus	Night-scented stock	Matthiola bicornis	Thistle	Cirsium		
Cactus	Cactaceae (astrophytum)	Orchid	Cattleya	Thrift	Armeria		
Calamint	Satureja calamintha	Poppy	Papaver	Water betony	Stachys		
Caraway	Carum carvi	Radish	Raphanus sativum	Water lily	Nymphaea		
Carpet bugle	Ajuga reptans	Rhubarb	Rheum rhaponticum	Winter savory	Satureja montana		

Table 3
Botanical Names of Flowers and Herbs

Intent	Sight Color	Taste Flavor	Smell Scent	Touch Feeling	Chant Sound	Chant Pitch/Style	Chant Speed	Timing Moon
Desire								
Wealth	Gold	Burgundy	Saffron	Velvet	Gay-ah	Low, Resonant Hum Largo	Slow	New
Love	Emerald Green	Port Wine	Orange Blossom	Making Love	Yah-weh	Medium Flowing Legato	Medium/ Slow	New
Serenity	Light Blue	Flounder	Lavender	Gelatin	A-um	Low, Resonant Hum Largo	Very Slow	Any
General Healing	Grass-Green	Salt	Rose	Baby Skin	Aye-oh	Very High Wailing Spirituoso	Very Fast	Full
Attack	Red	Chili	Tobacco	Burlap	Ele-lu	High Sharp Staccato	Fast	New
Luck	Dark Blue	Oatmeal & Brown Sugar	Narcissus	Cuddling	Aye-oh-em	High Sharp Staccato	Fast	New
Protection	Yellow	Butter	Night-Scented Stock	Waxed Wood	Homm	Medium Flowing Legato	Medium	New

Table 4
Mind Triggers for Seven Intents

Intent/Desire	Crystal	Mineral	Wood
Wealth	Gold	Gold	Teak
Love	Rose Quartz	Platinum	Heather
Serenity	Emerald	Silver	Willow
General Healing	Fire Opal	Copper	Olive/Rowan
Attack	Bloodstone	Iron	Ash
Luck	Rutilated Quartz	Tin	Locust
Protection	Black Tourmaline	Steel	Yew

Table 5
Natural Sources of Energy for Seven Intents

LEGAL IMPLICATIONS OF JOINING A WITCH GROUP[1]

The Church of Wicca[2] espouses the religion of Witchcraft as a spiritual path. Despite the fact that the Craft is federally recognized, still many people get into trouble when they commit actions in the name of Wicca (for example, healing, prediction, and others) before they protect themselves fully with the necessary legal documentation. Legal protection proves to authorities and to would-be nay-sayers that they are working within the guidelines of a legal, valid religion. When you use the power or take other Wiccan actions as a solitary, you are not likely to have any mundane problems; however, most of us eventually want to join a group to share experiences with like-minded people.

All over the nation, in such things as divorce cases, women are being harassed and are losing custody battles because the vindictive husband claims "She's a Witch (gasp!) and should not be allowed to raise *my* children." If you join a Wiccan group, make sure that it has

---

[1]Previously published in *The Witch's Magical Handbook*.
[2]In this Appendix, *Church of Wicca* means specifically the body founded by Gavin and Yvonne Frost in 1968.

done its paperwork with the IRS, that it's not just a couple of flakes who think they're cute claiming to be a church. If they claim to be affiliated with the Church of Wicca, ask to see their paperwork. If they can produce any, look carefully for an expiration date.

These are serious matters. Like any other human activity, the Craft is vulnerable to fools and charlatans. Don't be taken in.

There are two aspects of the Craft as spiritual path.

1. The spiritual/psychic/magical things you do for yourself and maybe for others.

2. The mundane/temporal side. To avoid hassles with the authorities and with people who don't want the Craft to exist, before you purport to heal or counsel, *make sure* any group you are associated with:

   A. Has done its paperwork with the IRS;

   B. Is registered with your state, your county, and your city.

A Non-profit Corporation Does Not a Church Make

Many people who are otherwise intelligent form the Church of XYZ as a non-profit organization (probably a non-profit *corporation*) and believe then they can safely do all the things that a conventional church can do—as they say in Europe, buryings, marryings, and healings. That assumption is false. A church is a different kind of beast, and if it is to earn recognition and tax-exempt status from the federal government, it must be able to meet the IRS guidelines. The IRS says:

> To exempt churches, one must know what a church is. Congress must either define 'church' or leave the definition to the common meaning and usage of the word; otherwise, Congress would be unable to exempt churches. It would be impractical to accord an exemption to every corporation which asserted itself to be a church. Obviously Congress did not intend to do this. *De La Salle*

Institute vs U.S., 195 F.Supp. 891, 903 (N.D. Cal. 1961).

The Tax Court carried that concept further in *Chapman vs Commissioner, 48 T.C. 358* (1967) when it determined that Congress used 'church' more in the sense of a denomination or sect than in a generic or universal sense.

Consistent with these principles, the Service does not accept any and every assertion that an organization is a church. We have adopted a ruling position based on historical and practical considerations in arriving at what the Court in De La Salle called 'the common meaning and usage' of the word 'church'. As important as these historical and practical considerations, however, have been our attempts over the years to isolate and distill from authoritative judicial sources those indicia of the existence of a church that are the most objective and least involved with particular beliefs, creeds or practices. But beliefs and practices vary so widely that we have been unable to formulate a single definition. The determination whether a particular organization is a church must, therefore, be made on a case-by-case basis. It may be helpful to list the characteristics we utilize:

(1)   a distinct legal existence

(2)   a recognized creed and form of worship

(3)   a definite and distinct ecclesiastical government

(4)   a formal code of doctrine and discipline

(5)   a distinct religious history

(6)   a membership not associated with any other church or denomination

(7)   a complete organization of ordained ministers ministering to their congregations

(8)   ordained ministers selected after completing prescribed courses of study

(9)   a literature of its own

(10) established places of worship

(11) regular congregations

(12) regular religious services

(13) Sunday schools for the religious instruction of the young

(14) schools for the preparation of its ministers

These requirements must be included and defined in the SOP (standard operating procedures) of any group proposing to earn recognition as a church. The IRS readily concedes that not all churches meet all its criteria; however, when a body does not meet one of its criteria, the proposers must explain the discrepancy.

Recognition of the Church of Wicca

In 1972 the Church of Wicca earned tax-exempt status as a religious association. Since that time the Church has fought an uphill battle for popular recognition as a valid (non-dangerous, though not Christian) church. The battle reached a high point in the Federal Appeals Court of Virginia.

In 1985 in Virginia a judge ruled that inmates who practiced Wicca must be allowed to have white robes, timers, candles, salt, and statuettes. In 1985 in *Dettmer vs Landon*, pursuant to rule 52(a) of the Federal Rules of Civil Procedure, the district court of Virginia ruled that Witchcraft is a legitimate religion and falls within a recognizable religious category. In 1986 the Federal Appeals court, fourth circuit, Judge J. Butzner affirmed this ruling in *Dettmer vs Landon (799F.2d 929)*. The affirmation clearly sets Wicca as a religion under the protection of constitutional rights. It stated:

> The Church of Wicca is clearly a religion for first amendment purposes. Members of the church sincerely adhere to a fairly complex set of doctrines relating to the spiritual aspects of their lives, and in doing so they have ultimate concerns in much the same way as followers of more accepted religions.

In most cases Federal law supersedes state law in this type of matter. As a result Wiccans everywhere are to some extent protected.

Be aware that the Church of Wicca founded by the Frosts is the only Wiccan church that has such an endorsement.

Healing and the AMA

The American Medical Association (AMA) is gradually coming to accept the idea that a link exists between mind or spirit and body.

Still you cannot go out and safely do herbal or psychic healing unless you have a doctor's license on the wall. Subsidiary or ancillary licenses such as nurse practitioner may let you scrape by. To be a psychic and herbal healer without AMA approval, the only avenue is to be a minister of a federally recognized legal church, healing *only parishioners of record in good standing in that same church. In good standing* means that the parishioner has been an active member of the church for many months.

Warning

When word gets out that you have investigated the Craft and its practices, many people will ask you for help. You must not help them, even unofficially, until:

1. You are a minister of a church recognized by the IRS; and

2. The person seeking help becomes a legitimate member of that church.

The United States has become such a litigious nation that if the least little thing goes wrong based on your advice, you will end up in court. Sorry, troops. That's the way it is.

Summary—Cover Your A++

In summary: If you want to be a church, go ahead and do the paperwork. If you want to join any alternative church, ask to see their paperwork. Once you are the minister of a church, treat and minister *only* to your own parishioners in good standing.

All this may sound paranoid—but it's only realistic to acknowledge a sad fact: There are many people who eagerly await an opportunity to dance on the grave of the Frosts and indeed of all Witches. Don't give them grounds to do so. In the words of that cynical precept,

Living well is the best revenge.

Index of
Tables, Figures,
and Work Sheets

TABLES

II-1	Example of Options and Visions	30
IV-1	Typical Power Needs for a Successful Ritual	57
VI-1	Measures for Tools and Circles	88
VI-2	Numerological Value of Letters	92
VII-1	Modern Dates Assigned to Each House	111
VII-2	Table of Dawn Times	114
VIII-1	Incantations to Charge and Reinforce the Gods of the Six Directions and Your Sphere of Protection	135
IX-1	God/esses for Seven Intents	145
IX-2	Circle Sizes	146
IX-3	Dimensions in Feet for Inner Circles	147
XII-1	Alternative Names for Segments of the Saturn Spiral	189
XII-2	Interlocking Cycles of Life and Ritual (2001)	190

FIGURES

I-1	Feeling Your Own Power	3
I-2	Your Magic Wand	6
I-3	The Star Position	8
I-4	Series Gives Maximum Force	10
I-5	Diadic Force	11
IV-1	Energy Spillover Effect	66
VI-1	The Athame Blade	90
VI-2	The Guard	90
VI-3	Signs Engraved on Blade of Athame	91
VI-4	Handle of Athame	91
VI-5	Calculating Your Name Number	92
VI-6	Leak Plug	95
VI-7	Siphoning Mead	95
VII-1	Full Moon	106
VII-2	New Moon	106
VII-3	Quarter Moons	107
VII-4	Monthly Variations in Moon Power	108
VII-5	Typical Daily Moon Variation	109
VII-6	Energy from Beyond the Stars	112
VII-7	Your Energy Power Dial	112
VIII-1	Your Mirror of Protection	131
VIII-2	Symbols and Colors of the Gods of Six Directions	134
VIII-3	Your Protective Headband	137
VIII-4	Ring of Protection—Example	138
IX-1	Ritual Circle	147
IX-2	Constructing the Cosmic Egg	150
IX-3	Levels of Excitement versus Ritual Sequence	152
IX-4	Section of Your RAPT Chart	155
X-1	Ritual Circle with Three Gates Closed	170
XII-1	The Saturn Cycle	188

WORK SHEETS

I-1	Testing Your Power	4
I-2	The Interruption Experiment	6
I-3	Testing the Effect of Fasting and Celibacy	13
II-1	Prioritizing	20
II-2	Your Options and Visions	30
III-1	Assessing the Quality of Your Life	41
III-2	Your Ten-Year Plan	47
IV-1	Your Guide to Power and Timing	62
IV-2	Your Correspondences Between Diseases and Colors	64
IV-3	Your First Ritual Checklist	67
V-1	Your Anger Mind Keys	71
V-2	Your Ritual Mind Keys to Anger	73
V-3	Your Mind Keys for Seven-Plus Intents	74
V-4	Your List of Psychic Links	77
V-5	Your Ritual Object Energy Detector	82
VI-1	Assessing Possible Locations	103
VII-1	Work Sheet to Identify Time of Ritual	115
VII-2	Adjusting Your Circadian Clock	117
VIII-1	Companionship	124
VIII-2	Wealth	126
VIII-3	Healing	128
IX-1	Your Materials Check Chart	153
IX-2	Your Task Check Chart	154
XI-1	Effects of Ritual	183
XII-1	Group Evaluation Work Sheet	193
XII-2	A Ritual Plan for You and Your Group	200

İΠDEX

A

Adrenaline, and increasing power, 12-13

Affirmations, concise/specific wording of, 50-53, 69

Altar
construction of, 88
use in rituals, 148, 166-70

Amulets, 14
See also Talismans

Ancient era, rituals in, xxiii-xxiv

Ancient monuments
cosmic egg shape, 149-50
Megalithic Yard (MY), 87-88, 149

Animals, avoiding materials from, 86

Anklet, as protective talisman, 139

Apartment, power place in, 99

Astral travel, homeostatic state for, 13-14

Astroarchaeology, on ancient monuments, 87-88

Astrological signs
on athame blade, 91
energy source for, 111-13
meta-psychometric table, 110, 202-3
in ritual space, 147, 169

Astrology, 110-13
house in, 110-11
Koch calculations, 116-17
timing rituals, 73, 111-17

Athame
construction of, 87, 89-92
use in ritual, 165

Aura
and disease, 65
and initiation, 159-60

B

Bath, pre-ritual, 161-62
Belt buckle, as protective
    talisman, 139-40
Bioplasmic energy, 1, 97
Birth signs. *See* Astrological signs
Blood, writing in, 52
Bodily orifices, protection of,
    136-41
Book of Light, construction of, 93
Bowls
    construction of, 93
    use in rituals, 147, 167-68
Brain, protective talisman for,
    137-38
Bread, use in rituals, 170
Brushwood Folklore Center, 101-2

C

Caging rituals, 122, 176
Candle holders, 96
Candles, use in rituals, 96, 147,
    166-67, 170
Career
    change, 34-36
    decision-making about, 49-50
    as future goal, 48-49
Castaneda, Carlos, 98
Cathedrals and churches, measure-
    ment standard, 149
Celibacy, and increasing power,
    12-13
Cenotes, 144
Chalice, construction of, 93
Channeling
    benefits of, 31
    for decision-making, 31-33
Chanting
    to raise power, 13, 144, 168
    for specific intent, 205
Chi, 1

Circadian clock, correction of,
    117-18
Circles. *See* Ritual space
Cleaning tools. *See* Psychic cleans-
    ing
Colors
    -disease correspondence,
        64, 201
    tuning psychic system with,
        63-64
Coming-of-age rituals, xxiv
Commentaries (Caesar), 87
Companionship
    as future goal, 48
    and romance, 42
Companionship rituals, 122-24
    as caging rituals, 122, 176
    cautions about, 176
    intent, identifying, 123-24
    mundane techniques,
        23-24, 182
    red rose experiment, 55-56
Copper sulfate, 86*n*, 147
Cosmic egg shape, 149
Cosmic energy, inhaling, 7-8
Crookes radiometer, 4
Crystals, 78-80
    choosing stones, 78-79
    mining, 80
    to raise power, 144
    related to intents, 206
    wearing stones, 78, 80

D

Daily life, ritualization of,
    xxiii-xxiv, 189-91
Dance, to raise power,
    143, 168
Dawn times, table of, 114
Day people, 118
Dettmer vs. Landon, 210
Diadic Force experiment, 11
Deities. *See* Gods/goddesses

Disease
   and aura, 65
   -color correspondence, 64, 201
   holding on to disease,
      127-28, 176-77
   karma of, 127
   See also Healing rituals; Health
Distance, and telepathic
      communication, 57-60
Dreams
   for decision-making, 31
   forgetting dreams, 31
   stages of, 61-62
   and telepathic communication,
      55-56, 61-62
Drumming, 13
   and channeling, 32-33
Dyes, natural, 89

E

Earth, healing with ritual,
      28-29
Earth magic, 97
Earth sign, 167
Elements and directions, during
      rituals, 166-67
Emeralds, 78
Emotions
   emotional response and senses,
      71-72
   and health, 76
   negative, and ritual
      materials, 86-87
   and rituals, 26-27
   and soul pieces, 77
Endorphins, stimulation of,
      13-14, 169
Energy. *See* Psychic energy
Energy spillover effect, 66
Equinoxes, seasonal rituals, 118-19
Equipment for rituals. *See*
      Magician's tools
Ethics, Witch's ethic, 157-58
Eye makeup, as protection, 138

F

Family, intentional households,
      197-99
Fasting, and increasing power,
      12-13
Fault lines, as power site,
      97, 98, 101
Feelings
   senses and emotional response,
      70-72
   and tables of correspondence,
      72
Feet, protective talisman for, 139
Feng shui, 40, 101
Ferrous metals, avoiding, 87
Fire sign, 166
Flowers, botanical names, chart of,
      204
Fontanelle, 7
Force, 1
Future goals. *See* Life goals

G

Garments
   continuous thread
      construction, 87
   robe, 89
Gates, in ritual space,
      148, 165, 169
Gender
   and electrical polarities,
      10-11
   entering the circle, 164-65
   perfect pairs group, 9-11
Genital area, protection of, 139
Geomancy, 97-98
Glass, for chalice and bowls, 93
Glastonbury, 99, 149
Goals. *See* Life goals
God bargain
   elements of, 144-45
   during ritual, 168

Gods/goddesses
    calling to raise power,
        144-45
    relationship to intents, 145
Gods of the Six Directions, for
        protection, 133-36, 140
Golden Section, 149
Gravitational pull, sun versus
        moon, 105-6
Grounding, for meditation, 13-14

H

Handfasting, 175*n*
Hands
    dominant and secondary hands,
        79*n*
    protective talisman for, 138-39
Head, protective talisman for,
        137-38
Headbands, protective, 137-38
Healing rituals, 127-29
    intent, identifying, 127-29
    laying-on-of-hands, 28
    legal considerations,
        122, 211
    mundane technique,
        21-22, 25, 34-36
    nighttime for, 119
    and psychic links, 65-67
    and unknown patient,
        128-29
Health
    and emotions, 76
    See also Disease
Hearing
    and emotional response, 72
    and ritual objects, 73
Heart, protective talisman, 138
Hearth, of ritual space, 148
Herbs
    botanical names, chart of, 204
    psychic effects of, 81
    use in rituals, 81, 147, 165
Hex
    signs of, 129-30, 136
    See also Protection

Hills, as power sites, 98
Home
    moving, reasons for, 101
    power place in, 99
    protection of, 133-36, 140
    relocation as future goal, 47-48
House, astrological, 110-11
Human behavior, and phase of
        moon, 107
Human Earth Dynamo Effect
        (HEDE), 97
Hysteresis, 108

I

Initiation, pre/post ritual mindset,
        158-62
Intentional households, 197-99
Intent of rituals
    chanting for, 205
    for companionship rituals,
        123-24
    defining intent,
        18-20, 29-33, 176
    gods/goddesses relationship to,
        145
    of healing rituals,
        127-29, 176
    and mind keys, 74
    mind triggers for, 205
    non-reversible rituals, 176
    and strange results, 175-77
    wealth as, 125-27, 174
    wording of,
        50-53, 69, 175-76
Internal Revenue Service (IRS),
        tax exempt status of
        churches, 208-10
Intersections, as power place,
        98, 99

J

Jet lag, 117
Jewelry, protective talismans,
        136-40

K

Kava kava, 76
Kirilian photography, 2
Koch calculations, 116-17
Kohl, as protection, 138*n*

L

Law of Attraction, 27
Laying-on-of-hands, 27-28
Leaders
    actions during ritual, 164-71
    evaluation of, 193-95
    method of leadership,
        157-58
Legal aspects, of Wicca/rituals,
    102-3, 122, 194-95, 207-8
Ley Hunters Society (Watkins), 99
Ley lines, 98-99
Life goals
    career, 48-49
    dreams into reality, 37-46
    home preferences, 47-48
    prioritizing of, 18-20, 29-33
    quality of life assessment, 39-42
    relationships, 48
    relocating, 46-47
    and Saturn cycle, 188-89
    See also Intent of rituals;
        Universal quests
Life-maintenance rituals,
    189-90
Life phases, time span of,
    187-89
Location for rituals, 96-103
    evaluation of sites, 103
    with geomancy, 97-98
    in house or apartment, 99, 100
    legal protection for, 102-3
    with ley lines, 98-99
    with map dowsing, 98
    in national/state parks,
        99-100, 102

power places, types of,
    97, 98, 99
    See also Ritual space
Lottery winners, 39, 174-75
Love
    attracting with gemstone, 78
    See also Companionship;
        Companionship rituals

M

Magical techniques
    channeling, 31-33
    combined with mundane
        techniques, 35-36, 182-83
    dreaming, 31
    pendulum, 35
Magician's tools, 85-96
    athame, 89-92
    Book of Light, 93
    candles and candle holders, 96
    chalice and bowls, 93
    cleaning equipment, 96
    dimensions of, 87-88
    garment construction, 87
    illegal objects, 86
    magic wand, 5-6
    materials to avoid, 86-87
    mead, 94-95
    non-ferrous metals, 87
    ritual objects, 72-73, 76-82
    robe, 89
    secret name and number, 92
    substitutions for, 158
    swords, 87
    worksheet for rituals, 153
Magic wand
    construction of, 5-6
    power of, 6
Magnetic fields, and gender, 10-11
Makeup, as protection, 138
Map dowsing, finding power
    place, 98
Masons, 171

Mead, recipe for, 94-95
Measurements
    Golden Section, 149
    medieval cathedrals, 149
    Megalithic Yard (MY),
        87-88
    oval/cosmic egg shape,
        149-50
    of ritual space,
        146, 147, 148-50
    sacred hand, 88
    standard hand, 88
Medicine bags, 81
Medieval buildings, measurement
    standard, 149
Meditation, homeostatic state for,
    13-14
Megalithic Yard (MY)
    construction of ancient monu-
        ments, 87-88, 149
    and Golden Section, 149
Metals
    athame, construction of,
        87, 89-92
    for circles of ritual space, 146
    metal ore as ritual object, 80
    non-ferrous metals, 87
Mind keys, 63-64, 69-76
    and focus, 70-72
    and intent of ritual, 74
    and ritual objects,
        72-73, 76-82
    senses and psychic responses,
        70-72
    tables of correspondences,
        64, 70, 201-6
Minerals, related to intents, 206
Mirror, protective mirror,
    131-32, 141
Mnemotechnics, 88
Money. See Wealth
Monkey law, xxii-xxiii
Moon phases, 107-10
    and human behavior, 107
    and planting, 106, 107
    and position of sun, 106-7

power variations, monthly and
    daily, 108-9
wane and wax, significance of,
    107-8, 109
zenith, 108
Moon sign, 166
Mundane forces, 130
Mundane techniques,
    21-29, 141-42
combined with magical
    methods, 35-36
for health, 21-22, 25, 34-36
for new relationship, 23-24
planning of, 190-91
for protection, 26
purpose of, 22
for serenity, 25-26
for wealth, 23, 29

Π

Native Americans, medicine bag,
    78
Navel, protective talisman for,
    139-40
Necklace, as protective
    talisman, 138
Night people, 118
Non-return rituals, 176, 185
Numerology, of secret name, 92

O

Orgasm, and homeostatic state, 14
Oval, cosmic egg shape,
    149-50

P

Parks, as ritual site, 99-100, 102
Pendulum, for decision-making,
    30-31

Pentagram, measurement standard, 149
Perfect pairs group, 9-11
Photographs
    and protective mirror, 131
    as ritual object, 77-78
    taboo and culture, 77
Place magic, 97
Planting, and phase of moon, 106, 107
Power
    and celibacy, 12-13
    and circadian clock, 117-18
    and day versus night people, 118
    and fasting, 12-13
    inhaling cosmic energy, 7-8
    levels during day, 3-4
    and magic wand, 5-6
    output during rituals, 152
    and perfect pairs group, 9-11
    raising power, methods for, 143-44, 168
    and stressors, 12-13
    testing your power, 2-4
    tuning power, 9
Power places, types of, 97, 98, 99
Prana, 1
Protection, 129-41
    of bodily orifices, 136-40
    of brain and head, 137-38
    of feet, 139
    of genital area, 139
    Gods of the Six Directions symbol, 133-36
    of hands, 138-39
    of heart and throat, 138
    of home, 133-36, 140
    mundane technique, 26
    of navel, 139-40
    from out-of-control forces, 130
    protective mirror, 131-32, 141
    psychic attack, signs of, 129-30, 136

psychic attackers, traits of, 140
Psychic attack
    attackers, traits of, 140
    signs of, 129-30, 136
Psychic cleansing
    procedure for, 96
    of ritual space, 100
    smudging, 100, 164, 167
Psychic energy
    bioplasmic energy, 1, 97
    and dwelling place, 101
    human output. *See* Power
    names for, 1
    place/earth magic, 97
Psychic links
    objects as, 77-78
    and telepathic communication, 65-67
Psychic responses, and senses, 70-72
Psychic vampires, effects of, 14

Q

Quality of life
    assessment of, 39-42
    versus wealth, 44-45

R

RAPT (Ritual Action, Planning, and Timing chart), 155-56
Record keeping, Book of Light, 93
Rede, for Witch's ethic, 157
Relationships. *See* Companionship; Companionship rituals
Religious service, definition of, xx-xxi
Relocation, as future goal, 46-47
REM (rapid eye movement), dream state, 62

Results of rituals, 173-85
    magic combined with reality,
        35-36, 182-83
    success, examples of,
        20-22, 59-60, 63, 75-76,
        109-10, 132-33, 174-75,
        178-80, 182-83
    timing of changes,
        177-78, 183-85
    unexpected results,
        27, 42, 52, 55-56,
        79-80, 175-81
Reversibility, non-reversible
    rituals, 176, 185
Ring, as protective talisman,
    138-39
Rite, definition of, xxi
Ritual objects, 72-73, 76-82
    crystals, 78-79
    herbs, 81
    metal ore, 80
    personal possessions of
        subject, 77
    photographs as, 77-78
    and senses, 73
    testing energy of, 81-82
    wearing, 78, 80
    wood, 80
Rituals
    affirmations in, 50-52
    cautions related to, 27, 69
    changes from. See Results of
        rituals
    and daily life, xxiii-xxiv, 189-91
    definition of, xxi
    and distance, 57-60
    and emotion, 26-27
    gender balance of group,
        9-11
    to heal Earth, 28-29
    and initiation, 158-60
    leadership for, 157-58
    location for, 96-103
    longest/shortest time for
        preparation, 155-56
    magician's tools, 85-96

meditative state for, 13-14
and mind keys, 63-64, 69-76
mood of, 164
mundane type,
    22-26, 190-91
parts of, 50, 150-51, 162-63
planning of, xxi, 152-56
prioritizing goals for,
    18-20, 29-33
procedure, master format for,
    163-72
purpose of. See Intent of
    rituals
ritual space, 145-50
timing of, 61-62, 73, 105-20
and Witch's ethic, 157-58
Ritual space, 145-50
    circle of containment,
        145-46
    circle of protection, 145-47
    circles during rituals,
        164-71
    cleansing, 100
    dimensions of circles,
        88, 146, 147
    gates, 148, 165
    hearth, 148
    measurement standards,
        146, 147, 148-50
Rivers, as power site, 98
Robe, design and construction
    of, 89
Romance, 42
Rose quartz, 78

S

Sacred hand, 88
Sage. See Smudge stick
Salt, use in rituals,
    86n, 147, 169
Samhain, date of, 118-19
Santería, 144
Saturn cycle, 188-89

Scrying, 78
Seasonal festivals, 118-19
Secret name
    on athame blade, 91
    numeric value of, 92
Secular rituals. *See* Mundane
        techniques
Selye, Hans, 12
Senses
    development of, 75
    and emotional response,
        70-72
    orientation and rituals, 73
Serenity, mundane technique,
        25-26
Serial applications, 154
Seven years, as life phase,
        187-88
Shamans, crystal use, 78
Silence, law of, 174-75
Smell, and emotional response,
        71-72
Smudge stick, 86
    cleansing ritual participants,
        164
    cleansing ritual space,
        100, 167
Snake, image in meditation, 49-50
Solstices, seasonal rituals,
        118-19
Soul pieces, 77
Spell, definition of, xxi
Springs, as power site, 98
Standard hand, 88
Star Position, inhaling cosmic
        energy, 7-8
Stone, Dr. Loy, 10
Stonehenge, 99, 148
Stressors, and increasing power,
        12-13
Sulfur, use in rituals,
        86, 147, 165, 169
Sun, position and phase of moon,
        106-7
Sun sign, 166
Sunday morning, and psychic
        energy, 3

Sunwise direction, 164-65
Swords. *See* Athame
Sympathy magic, 77

✝

Tables of correspondences,
        64, 70, 201-6
    personal tables, construction of,
        70-72
Talismans, for protection of body,
        136-41
Talk-out, example of, 49-50
Taste, and emotional response, 72
Tax-exempt status, of churches,
        208-10
Telepathic communication
    and distance, 57-60
    in dreams, 55-56, 61-62
    and psychic links, 65-67
Third eye, protection of, 137
Throat, protective talisman, 138
Tides, and sun and moon,
        106, 107, 108
Timing of rituals,
        61-62, 73, 105-20
    astrological method,
        73, 111-13
    evaluation of date, 113-16
    for healing rituals, 119
    and moon phase, 107-10
    for psychic energy output,
        117-18
    seasonal festivals, 118-19
Toning, 21
Touch, and emotional response, 72
Tuning psychic system, and mind
        keys, 63-64

U

Undergarments, protection from,
        139

United Nations building, 149
Universal quests
    for companionship, 122-24
    for health, 127-29
    for protection, 129-41
    for wealth, 125-27

V

Vision
    and emotional response, 71
    and ritual objects, 73
Vril, 1

W

Water sign, 167
Watkins, Alfred, 99
Wealth, 125-27
    intent of ritual, identifying,
        125-27
    mundane technique, 29
    "need" for, 23, 121
    results of rituals, example,
        174-75

rituals and phase of moon,
    107-8, 110
versus quality of life, 44-45
Wheater, Tim, 21-22
Wicca
    Church, legal implications,
        207-11
    group work, 192-95
Wine, use in rituals, 170
Witches, fear of, 129
Wood
    for altar, 88
    for chalice and bowls, 93
    handle of athame, 91-92
    and intent of ritual, 206
    as ritual object, 80
Wright, Frank Lloyd, 149

Y

Yarmulke, 137

Z

Zenith, moon, 108